Previous books by Richard Fisch

Change: Principles of Problem Formation and Problem Resolution
(coauthor with Paul Watzlawick and John Weakland)

The Tactics of Change: Doing Therapy Briefly
(coauthor with John Weakland and Lynn Segal)

Brief Therapy with Intimidating Cases

Richard Fisch
Karin Schlanger

Brief Therapy with Intimidating Cases

Changing the Unchangeable

WITHDRAWN

Jossey-Bass Publishers
San Francisco

Jossey-Bass books and products are available through most bookstores. To contact Jossey-Bass directly, call (888) 378–2537, fax to (800) 605–2665, or visit our website at www.josseybass.com.

Substantial discounts on bulk quantities of Jossey-Bass books are available to corporations, professional associations, and other organizations. For details and discount information, contact the special sales department at Jossey-Bass.

For sales outside the United States, please contact your local Simon & Schuster International Office.

 Manufactured in the United States of America on Lyons Falls Turin Book. This paper is acid-free and 100 percent totally chlorine-free.

Library of Congress Cataloging-in-Publication Data

Fisch, Richard, date.
    Brief therapy with intimidating cases: changing the unchangeable/Richard Fisch, Karin Schlanger.—1st ed.
        p. cm.
    Includes bibliographical references and index.
        ISBN 0-7879-4364-9 (alk. paper)
    1. Brief psychotherapy. I. Schlanger, Karin. II. Title.
RC480.55.F567 1999
616.89'14—dc21   98-36779
                                                                                                    CIP

FIRST EDITION
HC Printing   10 9 8 7 6 5 4 3 2 1

Contents

Preface

For thirty years, we have conducted numerous workshops and seminars on working with problems briefly. In the course of these presentations, participants frequently ask us a rhetorical, but also searching, question, which usually sounds something like this: "I've used your approach, and it often works beautifully. But can you really use it for serious cases such as psychoses?"

The question came as a surprise at first, because we have used our approach successfully in cases that would be called serious and that many therapists find intimidating. Then we realized that for the purpose of making our approach clear, we had usually used examples of less dramatic problems: marital conflict, parenting problems, anxiety, moderate depression, phobias, and the like. We also realized that the traditions of conventional therapy are very tenacious, especially the viewpoint of individual psychopathology. We felt that it was time to make clear that whatever the undesired behavior, however intimidating or serious, it is nevertheless *behavior*. Thus, the idea for this book was born.

THE CLIMATE FOR BRIEF THERAPY IN THE SIXTIES

Many readers may not remember what the climate was for brief psychotherapy thirty or more years ago. Psychotherapy (i.e., "healing talk"), largely as a result of the development and flourishing of psychoanalysis, had established itself as a legitimate means of alleviating people's distress. Although psychoanalysis was a relatively brief form of treatment at its inception (a six-month analysis with Freud and his contemporaries was not at all unusual), it became more elaborate, and in short order it evolved into a rather long venture for the patient, usually measured in years.

Concerned by this trend, a number of analysts (Alexander and French, Malan, Sifneos) attempted to find ways of shortening treatment. Because the psychoanalytic model itself was established as the legitimate view regarding people's troubles, innovators attempted to shorten therapy by abbreviating the technique of psychoanalysis while retaining its fundamental premises. A basic premise was that whatever the patient's complaint today, it is but a superficial manifestation of a rather complex state of affairs that had developed over time within the psyche of the patient. Further, this state of affairs was beyond the conscious awareness of the patient; its elements resided in the depths of the unconscious. Therefore, to consider any permanent alleviation of a patient's distress without reordering this unconscious state of affairs was regarded as pure naïveté if not charlatanism.

This was the predominant climate of psychotherapy thirty years ago. If a therapist reported a successful case after addressing only the patient's complaint, this success was discounted in a variety of ways: the change would not last, and the original symptom would return; a substitute symptom would surface, a symptom possibly even worse than the original (in my residency training some forty years ago, I remember being told, "Where there was an hysteric, you will see a schizophrenic!"); the original complaint was not *really* a phobia (or whatever the condition) but a more superficial matter, one amenable to "supportive" therapy. Thus, the therapist's focusing only on the patient's statement of distress or problem was discouraged; in short, problem-focused therapy was suspect, and it remained on the periphery of psychotherapy or was discounted altogether.

THEORETICAL ORIGINS OF PROBLEM-FOCUSED THERAPY

When we started our project, the Brief Therapy Center (sometimes known as the Palo Alto Group), in 1966 we knew we were flying in the face of convention by working with the client's stated complaint as the focus of therapy and not looking for "deeper" causes of his distress. We did not think of it as reckless, as we were following in the footsteps of a number of imaginative and solid innovators.

Many decades before, Harry Stack Sullivan broke new ground by viewing mental illness as an interpersonal phenomenon. (See H. S. Perry's Introduction in Sullivan, 1962.) In the 1940s, Gregory Bateson, together with the psychiatrist Jurgen Ruesch, had been interested in viewing psychiatric problems from a communicational standpoint (Ruesch and Bateson, 1951). Bateson, along with Don Jackson, Jay Haley, and John Weakland, brought this interest to further fruition in their study of communicational patterns within the families of people labeled as schizophrenic. Their work was the precursor of family therapy.

Prior to the efforts of Bateson and his colleagues, Milton Erickson, a psychiatrist in Phoenix, had for years been working with patients in a manner that discarded the notion of individual psychopathology. He put clients' troubles into a more human form; he conceived of these problems as understandable strivings in everyday life but strivings that had gone wrong (Haley, 1973).

What we are describing, then, is a long line of investigators of human difficulty who moved steadily away from the traditions of psychopathology and into the broader realm of social interaction. We saw our own work as following that pathway and building on the contributions of numerous others. Of them all, we would say we were most influenced by Erickson's work. We were attracted by his custom of assigning tasks, "homework," to patients and by his engagement in an active dialogue with them. We were also attracted yet at the same time mystified by the unique and unexpected twists of the tasks he gave people (e.g., asking a young man fearful of entering a restaurant to pick out a spot where he could best pass out).

In 1966, the Brief Therapy Center was formed to investigate a problem-focused approach to people's complaints and to evaluate results by means of follow-up interviews three months and one year after the last session. This book reflects our work with clients who have presented problems often intimidating to therapists, among them so-called serious problems, but also with clients so chronically impaired by their troubles that they seemed hopelessly enmeshed. It is more intimidating if clients seem to lack proper resources for working psychotherapeutically: if they are regarded as too concrete, lacking the capacity for "insight," or are struggling with fundamental life problems often imposed by poverty.

BRIEF THERAPY TODAY

Today, brief therapy is regarded as a legitimate achievement. Ironically, managed care is often credited with the introduction of brief therapy. Yet managed care is a beneficiary of those earlier efforts to shorten therapy, not the creator of shortened treatment. In a way, managed care both promotes and discourages brevity of treatment. On the one hand, it promotes brevity in the use of psychotherapy, but it does so by parceling out therapy sessions and challenging requests for additional sessions by requiring justification. On the other hand, it supports long-term treatment in its promoting of medication for patients. Thus, managed care finds it useful to support some models, mainly biochemical and genetic ones, because they allow for the less costly medicating of patients; monitoring medications requires much less professional time than does psychotherapy. These models declare that some problems are lifelong and will never be permanently resolved (e.g., Bipolar Disorder), and therefore treatment can last the lifetime of the patient. In the short run, using drugs can improve profits. Whether this will hold up in the long run is another question.

Although brief therapy has achieved respectable status, many therapists regard it as limited because of their assumption that although brief therapy can work well with the problems of everyday life (marital, child-rearing, sleep, or eating problems, even phobias and anxiety states, etc.), it cannot effectively deal with "serious" problems (schizophrenia, excessive drinking, severe depression, paranoia, etc.). For these so-called serious problems, biological explanations have become attractive, and referral to psychiatrists—with the attendant use of drugs as the primary treatment—has become more widespread.

OVERVIEW OF THE CONTENTS

The challenge of resolving serious or intimidating problems with brief therapy is the focus of this book, which we regard as a modest attempt to "open the door" to this challenge. It is not a statement of incontrovertible success in treating all serious problems but rather an offering of our experiences to show "it can be done" and to encourage like-minded researchers and clinicians to probe ahead beyond our own work.

In order to illustrate how a problem-solving approach can work with intimidating cases, we have presented cases that succeeded and show how this success was brought about. It might have been better to have included some of the many cases in which we failed, along with our best appraisal as to how we failed. We felt, however, that this might be material for a separate book.

For readers unacquainted with our earlier work (principally Watzlawick, Weakland, and Fisch, 1974; Fisch, Weakland, and Segal, 1982), Chapter One is a brief statement of our basic assumptions, but we also encourage you to refer to the original works cited. Chapters Two through Eight are devoted to different categories of intimidating problems we have worked with in the Brief Therapy Center as well as in our individual practices. Chapter Nine looks to the future with some few thoughts on where and how further investigation might go.

TRIBUTE TO JOHN WEAKLAND

There is another reason for writing this book. John Weakland, a cofounder of the Brief Therapy Center, died in 1995. More than a cofounder, he imparted a unique imagination and boldness to the project. He was totally unintimidated by challenges, and he met them with a thoroughness of investigation that was remarkable.

His interests were amazingly far ranging. Originally a chemical engineer, he felt that was not his niche. He gave up engineering and went back to school to study, of all things, anthropology. It was during those studies in New York that he met Gregory Bateson. Bateson later invited Weakland to join him in California, where he planned to study the communication within families that included a "schizophrenic" member. Weakland and his wife, Anna, packed up their things and came west. It was in that project that Weakland became committed to the concept of interaction.

His later projects included studying Chinese communist films to see what changes had occurred in portraying the expected roles of family members. He extended his interest in interaction into such areas as problems of the aged, health problems (coining the term *family somatics*), problems of organizational management, and nations' different styles of diplomatic negotiating; just before his death, he began studying developmentally disabled people who were working in a sheltered occupational program.

Weakland was enormously generous with his time. The door to his office was almost always open, and colleagues were able to consult or chat with him freely. Even in the last years of his life, when he was no longer able to go to his office, he welcomed friends and colleagues and continued consultations at his home. He managed to continue writing until he was unable to hold a pencil, but continued working with his ideas by dictating to a secretary.

The legacy Weakland has left is immeasurable and will probably never be fully appreciated. He was not what one would call a charismatic figure; he was modest, perhaps to a fault, but his energies were always devoted to his work and the continuing exploration of ideas. He shunned the seductive quest for image in a world increasingly oriented to image rather than substance.

This book is a small tribute to Weakland and his tenacity in challenging the "impossible." He referred to himself as curious, and in his painstaking efforts to elicit a clear description of exactly what troubles people were experiencing, he would demystify their problems, opening up options they hadn't imagined.

ACKNOWLEDGMENTS

As is the case with many works, this book did not simply arise from our own minds. We wish to express gratitude to the countless professionals whose interest in our work led to their challenging question regarding its application to intimidating or serious cases.

In particular, we wish to thank the steadfast collaboration in our work at the Brief Therapy Center of Barbara Anger-Diaz, also a loyal friend; Paul Watzlawick, who has stuck with us through thick and thin since the Center's inception; Lucy Gill, who expanded our horizons to the field of organizational management (Gill, 1999). We also wish to thank Teresa Garcia and Jean Jacques Wittezaele of the Gregory Bateson Institute in Liëge, Belgium; to many other colleagues abroad; and to Steve de Shazer and Insoo Kim Berg, who demonstrated the cross-cultural application of our work. To Wendel Ray, a man of tireless energy who encouraged our work through the years, we offer our thanks. Nor can we overlook the patient efforts of Phyllis Erwin, the administrator of the Mental Research Institute, who made our tasks easier by aiding us in overcoming the daily frustrations of organizational life. We also appreciate the care and efforts of our editor, Alan Rinzler, who helped keep us at it as well as providing very helpful suggestions for the manuscript. Finally, one of us (R.F.) wishes to express deep appreciation to a most loyal friend, Larry Spector, who selflessly and persistently gave of his time and energies to help me find my way through the computer and word processing mazes and whose constant encouragement spurred the attempt, finally, to sit down and write.

Palo Alto, California   RICHARD FISCH
January 1999   KARIN SCHLANGER

Introduction

How do problems come to be called serious or intimidating? Conventional wisdom would have it that by their very nature, certain problems are inherently resistant to methods successful in dealing with "unserious" problems. Explanations for that difference assume that elements of the problem lie within the individual whose behavior is being questioned. It is not uncommon for a therapist who attests to the validity of interactional concepts (e.g., family therapy) to abandon those concepts when confronted by a serious problem and to retreat to the traditional viewpoint of individual psychopathology, a monadic explanation.

If, for example, a therapist attempts to intervene in behaviors that are considered bizarre *and* intervenes only with the complained-about person (the client), *and* that person is not asking for help to change, then, when the therapy fails, the client is labeled as suffering from a serious problem, one that lies beyond the usual practice of psychotherapy. Failure is attributed to the client, not the approach taken.

In addition, the individual with an intimidating problem is regarded as significantly *different* from "normal" people because of some enduring pathology—genetic factors, or firmly entrenched mood, or a thought defect developed over time, or some unexplainable but nevertheless physical quirk within the person's mind (e.g., a vulnerability to alcohol, or stress, or whatever). All of these labels lend an aura of fixedness to the problem and implicitly discourage the therapist from anticipating beneficial change at the very start of contact with the client. A therapist confronted by schizophrenia, for example, is more likely to be pessimistic about the successful outcome of therapy, and this pessimism, of course, may be detrimental to the therapy just as optimism may be beneficial.

There are other features contributing to the notion of seriousness. A significant one is that the impact of the problem behavior is potentially catastrophic. A client may be considered as having a mild depression unless he jeopardizes his own or, certainly, the family's financial structure by not working or by expressing plans to commit suicide. Then he is labeled as having a serious depression.

Thus, *serious* is likely to be a diagnostic term for behavior that exceeds the boundary of being annoying, inconvenient, embarrassing, and the like, and instead poses threats of suicide, homicide, assault, starvation, or economic disaster. Therapists also will consider a problem serious if a client is so dominated by his problem that he is nearly incapacitated. Patients who present multiple problems or who exhibit bizarre "symptoms" (such as self-mutilation) also intimidate many therapists.

Although it may seem naive, we have taken the view that problems are best defined as behaviors distressing to someone seeking change: the person has a complaint. The features of the behavior may differ from person to person, and the behavior complained about may vary depending on a number of factors. What a complaint comprises can be very idiosyncratic. What one person regards as a problem, another might regard as unexceptional. For us, *if there is no complaint, there is no problem*. This assumption departs from the traditional view that features of the problem behavior reflect an abnormal condition, illness, or disorder to which diagnostic labels are given.

Our viewpoint does not dismiss the idea that some behaviors can and have been catastrophic, but these remain, nevertheless, behaviors. In the traditional view, the therapist will organize information in an effort to arrive at a diagnosis, because she regards this as necessary to knowing how to intervene. She will then treat the *diagnosis*. In contrast, we make a careful assessment of the problematic behavior and then treat the *behavior*. For example, the traditional therapist asks, "What do you do about obsessive-compulsive disorder?" We ask, "What do you do with a person who checks the oven ten or more times before leaving the house?"

In Chapter One, we expand our discussion of the underlying assumptions of our work and how they determine our approach to addressing complaints. For a fuller description of our underlying rationale, we recommend reading *The Tactics of Change: Doing Therapy Briefly* (Fisch, Weakland, and Segal, 1982).

In memory of
John H. Weakland
and
Joyce Emamjomeh
past administrator of MRI

Brief Therapy with Intimidating Cases

1

Underlying Assumptions

In order to address a problem, to intervene, a therapist needs to operate on some body of assumptions, a model. The model may be simple or complex, but, in any case, it forms the guidelines of what to do and, equally, what not to do. In the field of psychotherapy, these assumptions are usually a "reality" constructed to explain what problems are about; in a manner of speaking, the model is an explanation for why people have problems or certain types of problems. (Some therapists will say they do not operate from any theory, but it is likely they are unaware of the guidelines that dictate their "moves" in therapy.) The following are our assumptions about problems and their implications for intervening.

NO COMPLAINT, THEN NO PROBLEM

We see problems as behaviors that someone strongly considers undesirable, rather than as manifestations of pathology. Thus, if no one is registering a complaint about a behavior, there is no problem. In that sense, our assumptions depart from concepts of normality and abnormality and, instead, are *complaint*-based.

We cast no judgment on the legitimacy of a complaint; everyone has his or her own standards of acceptable or unacceptable behavior. Although we may not, as individuals, share many of our clients' standards, we respect them as the vagaries of people's priorities and sensibilities. A complaint we might consider trivial has the same legitimacy for therapy as one we would consider catastrophic; by the same token, we accept a client's statement that a state of affairs, dreadful as it might seem to us, is not a problem for her or him. Thus, as you will see in subsequent chapters, with few exceptions we start the initial session by asking, "What is the problem that brings you in?" This question also alerts the client that her problem is the first and therefore the main order of business, centering therapy in the present.

THE ATTEMPTED SOLUTION IS PART OF THE PROBLEM

How a problem started is not significant to us. Instead, we regard as central to our model that problems, however they may have started, *persist* because of the persistent tack the complainant has been taking in his or her efforts to resolve the complaint; we call this tack the *attempted solution*. This idea is the principal factor in our assumptions or model. Thus the thrust of therapy is not to get the complainants to *do* something so much as to *stop* what they have been doing about the problem. In a manner of speaking, resolution is achieved by allowing the problem to dissipate rather than by exerting an effort to overcome it. In that sense, we would say that we don't treat problems, we treat attempted solutions. Nevertheless, we do offer alternative actions to clients on the basis that a person can't stop doing something without doing something else instead. (Try to stop sitting without taking a new action!)

We proceed with the idea that there is nothing special about clients who persist in a counterproductive mode. If we inquire about attempted solutions, they are, with few exceptions, expressions of everyday logic or common sense; for example, if someone is fearful about an ordinary task, say, entering a large building, it is a common impulse for helpful people to tell her, "There's nothing to be afraid of; everyone does it." Because such reassurance seems to be the only reasonable thing to say, friends or family persist, perhaps trying to put it in a different way: "Look. What's going to happen? Nothing!"

We think the examination of common logic would make for an interesting study. How is it that people get stuck on only one option? It seems very difficult for people to shift their frame of reference from "What is logical?" to "What works?" Concomitantly, it is most common for people not to realize they are doing the same thing over and over, merely in different forms.

For example, an acquaintance of ours had been hired by a family to tutor their ten-year-old son. At first the child maintained interest in the work, but as the tutoring went on, he would quickly lose interest and find all kinds of ways to resist or sabotage the tutor's efforts. He would maintain his focus when the tutoring involved play but not when the tutor tried to get him to concentrate on the needed work. The tutor found the job increasingly frustrating and began to dread coming to the family's home. She entertained the idea of quitting, but she needed the income. She felt she had tried everything and was about to give up. She had tried to limit his play with lessons; she explained that play interfered with the necessary work, that it wasn't good for him. She hoped to motivate him by offering the play activity as a reward at the end of the more formal lessons. None of these tactics succeeded.

Even though she felt she had tried everything, she was doing only one thing, albeit in different forms: she was depending on the message to him, "You must buckle down to work!" She mentioned that during one lesson, she was so exhausted trying to keep him on track that she interrupted the lesson to tell him, "You've had a long day, and I think you should stop the work and play." He quickly took her up on her offer, but after ten minutes he returned to the table where they had been working and seemed interested in resuming the lesson. Rather than continue with what worked—"You *shouldn't* buckle down to work"—she did what, to her, was logical: she attributed his renewed interest in the work as his recognizing her disapproving facial expression, and she reverted to "Good, let's get back to work." This comment didn't achieve the sustained effort she hoped for, and she again felt helpless.

We clearly delineated what didn't work and what did and made some suggestions as to how she could try out our different tack; the gist of it was, "You look tired [or you look like you've had a hard day], why don't you just play." Even though she reported that he stuck with the work significantly better than before and on some lessons accomplished a considerable amount of work, she said she found it difficult to maintain this tack with him because it seemed so illogical; besides, she attributed his concentrating on the work to his finally recognizing how much work there was to be done and how necessary it was. Considering that this woman is by no means stupid or stubborn, we are inclined to attribute her difficulty in departing from a counterproductive path to the difficulty in shifting one's frame of reference, that is, one's "reality."

INTERACTION IS CENTRAL

We believe that people in any ongoing contact with each other unavoidably influence each other. This belief is an essential element in interactional thought, one that is intrinsic to our view regarding the persistence of problems. Thus, whereas a client may regard his child's undesirable behavior as reflecting an internal or intrapsychic phenomenon, we look to the *interaction* between that parent and his child, especially those interactions revolving around the stated complaint.

For example, a parent says his child is a liar. If we inquire about the context in which the child lies, we find it is usually when he is confronted by some direct or indirect accusation by the parent, a confrontation with which the child deals by denying guilt. Because the parent suspects or believes the child is guilty, the interrogation will continue, often with heated exchanges, and the parent chalks up the episode as yet another example of the child being a liar.

Mainly, the complainant takes the linear view that the child's lying is something that he is simply inclined to do, instead of taking the interactional view that the child lies *in response to* the parent's interrogating him. It can be confusing to the parent if the therapist summarizes the exchange by saying that the child lies *when* he is interrogated and that, hypothetically, he would not lie if he weren't interrogated. Many parents will reply that, even though that is true, it is necessary to interrogate "to get the child to admit his guilt," as they deem his confession necessary to legitimize any punishment they give him.

This interactional viewpoint is most instrumental when the complaint is about another, as in the example of the lying child, and when that other does not acknowledge there is any problem. Here again, the parents are assuming that the child needs to be brought in "to cure him of his lying" rather than that they need to stop interrogating and to use other ways to justify imposing consequences.

CHANGE PROMOTES FURTHER CHANGE

Because we view problems as requiring continuing effort (the attempted solution) in order to be maintained, once a minimal but strategic change takes place, we expect further change will ensue in a ripple or domino effect. That is, once the client has begun to abandon his previous problem-maintaining efforts, a positive result will begin to manifest itself, which will in turn encourage him to depart further from the attempted solution, and so on. This ripple effect is one factor enhancing brevity of treatment. Often, therapy need not go the whole distance, as it were, but simply get the ball rolling.

DESCRIPTION, NOT DIAGNOSIS

Although this model is simple in its structure, implementing it in actual practice belies its simplicity. The model is counterintuitive; that is, it fundamentally departs from the traditions of psychotherapy. In most therapies, one must arrive at a diagnosis in order to determine the appropriate treatment: Is the complained-about behavior "depression" or "anxiety" or an "agitated depression" or "obsessive-compulsive" or . . . ? In contrast, our model requires the therapist to think in terms of *a description* of the complained-about behavior and of the attempts at solution.

Suppose, for example, that a parent says her child has yet to complete a day at school because he cries pitifully every morning when anticipating school, kicks and screams when being urged to go, and (if the parent succeeds in getting him to school) causes the parent to have to bring him back home at the school's request because his distress is disruptive to the class. The usual label (diagnosis) for this is Separation Anxiety Disorder (according to *DSM-IV*). This label tends to restrict the focus of intervention to the child, most often involving engaging the child in an effort to find out *why* he is anxious. Thus, little investigation is made to gain a fuller picture of the distressing behavior; for example, *in what context* does the child begin to cry or kick and scream or be disruptive in the class? Is it in response to the parent's reassuring him that he has nothing to be fearful of, that he will have a good time? Because of previous episodes, does the teacher say or do something in anticipation of his disruptive actions to which his behavior is a response? and so on.

In addition, diagnostic labels can implicitly impose an expectation of unchangeability, of pessimism, on both the client and the therapist. The label "alcoholic" implies a fixedness and an expectation that the individual must make fundamental changes, whereas the phrase "She drinks more than is desired" avoids this intimidating expectation. In the first case the client expects that she will have to become a different person; in the second, she needs to find a way to stop an undesired action.

In essence, our model departs from focusing on what to label an undesired behavior and instead focuses on thinking about how and in what context the undesired behavior is *performed*. This latter idea tends to be overlooked by professionals because the traditions of Western healing methods have established diagnosis (boxes) as a sine qua non for proceeding.

In Chapter Two, we begin illustrating the application of these assumptions by looking at a type of problem usually regarded as intimidating because it involves a life-threatening state, one in which the client is regarded as having departed from reality: severe depression.

2

Severe Depression

On the one hand, therapists are unlikely to feel intimidated by cases in which the client is complaining about feeling depressed but is still working or functioning at a reasonable (albeit lower than desired) level. Even in these cases, however, if therapy is not making the inroads hoped for, therapists will often refer the client to a psychiatrist, who is likely to prescribe drugs. Referral is especially likely if the client should threaten suicide. (Sometimes, if the client still does not show progress, the therapist will assume that the dosage or kind of medication is insufficient, whereas the psychiatrist may question the therapy. Most likely, the psychiatrist will readjust the medication, and the therapy will continue as before.)

When the therapist regards a client as being seriously depressed, she can find the case quite intimidating; she is more likely both to make a referral to a psychiatrist and to refer sooner in the therapy. The therapist may also assume that strong measures are required: medication, hospitalization, and electric shock treatment are highlights of this kind of intervention. The client's threats of or attempts at suicide reinforce this full-scale approach.

By *severe depression* we mean those episodes in which an individual, while expressing a low mood, behaves in a way that significantly interferes with fundamental activity such as work or school or that jeopardizes his health because of poor sleep, loss of appetite and weight, or diminished hydration. We use this definition to distinguish these behaviors from those of people who are depressed but who manage to sustain important activities and care of their basic health. This distinction is a strategic one, because diminished health and the decline of activities that define a person's role can in turn intensify that person's feelings of depression. An individual may stop working because of feeling depressed, but her ceasing work can be depressing in itself, thus producing a vicious cycle.

When an individual is behaving in the manner we have described as seriously depressed, the complainant is usually a relative, such as the spouse, rather than the depressed person himself or herself. The case in this chapter involved such an arrangement; the treatment team saw the depressed husband only once. (This case was treated in the Brief Therapy Center; the primary therapist works in conjunction with the members of the team, who observe through a one-way mirror. Because of the research element of the Center's work, we operate within a ten-session limit.)

Traditionally, even when the therapist sees a spouse first, the spouse is often regarded as a kind of bystander, a helpless victim of her husband's "illness." Information she gives is considered important for the purpose of making or confirming a diagnosis in preparation for treating the patient. As we have already discussed, we view the complainant as the more strategic person in therapy: it is the complainant who is making the most concerted efforts to change a situation but whose efforts we regard as unwittingly *maintaining* the very problem he or she is trying to change. We mention that again here so that you will not assume we focused on Miriam rather than Al because he was hospitalized, nor be puzzled about why we had such minimal contact with the "real patient." (As with all cases in this book, the names and identities of the participants are fictitious.)

MIRIAM AND AL

Miriam came to the Center because of her concern about her husband, Al, who she said was seriously depressed. He was sixty-five, she sixty-two. He retired from his business following a heart attack, and they moved to this area because their daughter and son-in-law lived out here. Al had been taking an antidepressant, but it was not helping; when he implied he might commit suicide, his psychiatrist strongly suggested Al enter the hospital. At the time of the first interview with Miriam, he had been hospitalized a week. Miriam added that he had been depressed in the previous year, was hospitalized for six weeks, and received electric shock treatment at that time. Another previous episode of depression occurred two years before; he was hospitalized for three to four weeks but did not receive electric shock treatment.

Miriam said that his getting depressed seemed to start with his preoccupation that they wouldn't have enough money to live on; he feared that they would be evicted from their apartment and that they and their belongings would be out on the street. The tenacity of this belief, the omnipresence of his preoccupation, made her all the more frightened.

Session One

In the first session, we met with Miriam and her daughter, Sara. In all, nine weekly sessions constituted the treatment.

> THERAPIST: *(To Miriam)* What's the problem?
> MIRIAM: Well . . . after the heart attack. He had his own business where he had to physically work very hard. So after his heart attack he gave his business up. He was actually looking forward to it and moving to California because our daughter lives in California. . . . We rent an apartment in San Francisco, and for a while he seemed pretty good, and then he started to worry

about the financial aspect. "Oh," he said, "we made a mistake. Things are expensive here. We're not going to make it."

I assured him that we do make it. And lately he did not want to spend any money on anything 'cause he said we cannot afford it. That is his main problem, that he is worried about how we're going to make it. But I told him with his Social Security and my Social Security and a little savings we will be able to make it. I assured him. And my son-in-law figured it out with him on paper over and over again, and each time he says, "We won't be able to pay the rent and then they're going to remove the lease; our furniture will be out on the street." He was telling me horrible things all the time. And I told him it isn't so. (*Miriam had also mentioned that, while in the hospital, Al had said his phone was bugged.*)

THERAPIST: And I take it then that things grew worse?

MIRIAM: It grew worse, yeah.

THERAPIST: What actually led up to his hospitalization? The present one I mean.

MIRIAM: The present one, I tell you. Last Wednesday we went shopping, and I bought very little. He seemed to be very angry with what I bought. And then we came home and he didn't even take his coat off. Then, in the evening he wanted to go out, and I said, "Where are you going?" He said, "I don't know. I just wanted to go out."

And so I called my daughter and son-in-law, and while I was talking with him she went to the other phone and called Dr. M., and he said to bring him to the hospital. Then Al told me he figured that if he would go away, there would be enough money for me, and I said, "Where would you go?" and he said, "I don't know."

THERAPIST: And this worried you?

MIRIAM: Yeah.

THERAPIST: So, I take it that in his view, the problem is the

shortness of money and the uncertain future. I see he is sixty-
five years old.

SARA: He has a lot of . . . if I can have some input at this
point, he has the classic symptoms of depression . . . feelings of
worthlessness, a lot of anxiety, many anxieties. He has a fear of
driving; he has a lot of anxieties other than just the financial situation.

This last comment by Sara illustrates the importance of recognizing the client's position. The therapist had just offered a summary
of the problem as Al's worry about money and the future. It would
appear that their daughter heard this as too superficial an understanding of her father's condition, and she felt it necessary to correct the record, what we would call stating a *position;* in this case it
is a pessimistic position to correct the therapist's optimistic one.

As a general rule, particularly in severe cases, the complainant
is likely to be feeling intimidated by the problem, feeling helpless,
if not hopeless; you should pay attention to the expression of that
pessimism. You can make little error by adopting an equally if not
more pessimistic stance. The main danger is in taking what would
appear to be an optimistic position. It runs the risk of leaving the
client with the feeling that you do not understand the seriousness
of her situation and can markedly reduce your credibility.

The therapist now shifted to obtaining a clear picture of Miriam
and Sara's attempted solution. We define attempted solutions as
those efforts people make with the specific goal of alleviating the
problem. Even though Miriam and Sara had already given several
examples of their efforts, mostly reassurances that they had enough
money, we prefer to have those efforts confirmed as well as explicitly established as efforts to change things.

THERAPIST: *(To Miriam)* How have you tried to deal with
this so far? How have you tried to help him?

MIRIAM: Most of the time I was patient. I told him, "Don't worry about anything." I said, "We'll be able to manage." I did try to push him to go to the senior citizen club. And while I was there they told me they were going to have a trip to Monterey. So I thought that would do him good to go. He said we cannot afford it, and I said, "Yes we can." And on the trip I commented on the landscape being beautiful, and he said he didn't enjoy it. I thought it would do him good, but he said he didn't enjoy it at all.

THERAPIST: *(To Sara)* How have you tried to help him?

SARA: Well, we've tried to be as supportive as possible. My husband has really put in a real amount of feeling and effort and energy in the areas where Dad is worried about finances. Dad really respects my husband in his ability in terms of business and so forth. He has always taken his counsel in terms of money affairs, so John has always tried to go over the financial situation, pointing out the realities of the situation.

Now that it has continued, I've done a little reading, a little talking with some friends who are psychologists, trying to inform ourselves a little better and I wonder . . . it seems like most of the things we've done are generally considered helpful, therapeutic. I think sometimes we have taken the wrong tack and tried to point out realities when maybe that was too stressful to him.

In a very succinct way, the daughter put, in a nutshell, the dilemma of many clients. That is, they will do what is generally considered correct (logical, realistic, therapeutic, right) even though it is not effective or even worsens the situation. They persist with it because it is regarded as the correct thing to do. That is their frame of reference, their reality. (One of the authors, R.F., recalls a high school biology lesson on instincts that the teacher illustrated with the example of a species of wasp that would laboriously persist in building a nest even though the bottom half had been destroyed; the wasp would abandon the nest on completion.)

THERAPIST: Like what sort of realities, for instance?

SARA: Well, driving is one of the big anxieties. . . . Until very recently I was basically a listener, supportive and sympathetic, and I could see that was not doing too much so this was one time when I was alone with him, and I decided to take a little more forceful tack and kind of hammered away at the fact that I had every confidence that he could drive. I tried to counter every one of his reasons. He would say the car needs a checkup, and I tried to say that even a jalopy twice its age could go around the block. Just put the key in the ignition; just go around the block and park it! That kind of very realistic thing.

It is quite common for clients to believe they have taken a different tack because they are saying the same thing but forcefully or softly. All along, both Miriam and Sara had been taking the tack, "You needn't worry; you can do it." Usually it had been in the "softer" way: reasoning, encouraging, urging. What Sara just described was her doing the same thing, but she regarded it as substantially different because she was being forceful in her expression.

THERAPIST: I take it that he manages to make all three of you [this includes the son-in-law] more optimistic than you would otherwise be perhaps . . . that he somehow has a way of bringing the two of you into pointing out to him that things, after all, aren't so bad . . . when he starts talking about how dreadful things are and that very soon you will be out on the street—

MIRIAM: Yes, I keep on telling him that he is wrong.

SARA: Yes, his pessimism is not quite justified.

It was already clear to the therapist that their well-meant efforts to help Al were backfiring and locking in his depressive stance. It was also clear that their well-meant efforts were mainly those of encouragement to feel and perform better. Here, the therapist made an attempt to redefine their efforts as part of a repetitious *interaction* between them and Al, with Al as much of an active participant in that interaction as they were.

This is a kind of "testing" intervention to see if the client will accept the redefinition and therefore question the appropriateness of her efforts. In this case, however, both wife and daughter continued with their original frame of reference, reiterating their justification of what they had been doing. The therapist quickly withdrew from his reframing and shifted to another approach:

> THERAPIST: What has Dr. M. suggested that you should be doing? Particularly when Al is out of the hospital and is back home?
> MIRIAM: He has not said anything.
> SARA: His approach seemed to be to get Dad to a better situation so that he could get therapy.

At the end of the first session, the therapist asked if they would check with Al's psychiatrist to allow Al to come to our Center. They said they would ask him.

Session Two

The second session was held with Miriam and Sara again. Because it was clear that their attempted solution was to reassure Al that he needn't worry about money and that he should become more active because he would enjoy himself, the therapist laid the groundwork for getting them to depart from that tack. He defined Al's pessimistic statements as metaphors; as such, Miriam and Sara's ordinary reasoning was unlikely to be effective. The therapist advised them to desist from making such comments.

> THERAPIST: We've done a lot of work with families in which, in addition to whatever treatment plan may be instituted

for a patient, we seek out ways that families can use resources that they may not have thought of using. . . . Usually in depression people are feeling rather badly about themselves, but your husband's bizarre statements nevertheless seem to contain an element very much other than self-belittling. . . . What might be occurring is that he is attempting to communicate, but in a way and on a level that if you attempt to respond reasonably, what I think is happening is that there is a cross-communication in which nothing gets across. . . . I'm saying that to get a better idea, in more understandable terms, of what you are concerned about might require all of you to hold off on applying the ordinary, everyday reasoning when he starts off with these crazy statements.

SARA: Uh huh.

The daughter had alluded earlier to her father's "other fears." Although Al expressed these other fears much less frequently, they had strongly contributed to Miriam and Sara's concern. It is one thing to go on about "We don't have enough money," but it is regarded as ominous that someone is accusing unknown others of persecution, a position usually regarded as delusional.

THERAPIST: So, instead of saying, as we ordinarily would do, "I doubt that," when he says, "You know, they're bugging my phone," . . . think of a different kind of question for the purpose of allowing him to elaborate a bit more, like, "What do you have in mind? If they are bugging your phone, what makes your conversation that interesting or important to listen in on?"

SARA: I have asked him a similar question: "Why would they pick on you?"

It is very common for a client to translate a therapist's comment into her own frame of reference, essentially missing the difference. Here, the therapist's comment avoided *challenging* the patient's contention that his phone was being bugged, asking instead what made his conversation of interest to others, whereas the daughter's comment was a challenge to Al's "delusional" thinking.

> THERAPIST: It may sound very picky in terms of communication, but if you have expressed some question about what he is saying and then you raise the question, "Well, why would they do that?" it is too close to "I do not believe it."
>
> SARA: Yeah. OK. I think that is true.
>
> THERAPIST: You are conveying something very different if you say, "What makes you so special that they would want to bug your phone?"
>
> MIRIAM: Uh huh.
>
> THERAPIST: Yes. It makes you curious. What I'm asking you to do will not be easy.

Session Three

In the third interview, the therapist saw only Sara and her husband, John. In the preceding week, Al had been discharged from the hospital, which they attributed to the effects of a new antidepressant. The therapist persisted with the previous tack, getting them to depart from their previous efforts of optimism and instead to adopt a cautionary pessimistic stance.

> THERAPIST: We had asked you to do something. I'm curious as to how it went.
>
> JOHN: I tried it. A lot of what he said was very much of how he usually is. The suspicion and stuff. He was always somewhat like that, and when he was in the hospital he thought he was being tested to see what was real and what was not because he had talked about suicide. In terms of the money and the phones, they were not necessarily out to harm him, but they were trying to find out whether he actually was crazy.

SARA: It was almost a crutch to build a conversation around. I found it useful.

JOHN: There definitely was a lot more harm in trying to win the argument, and this led to much more of a conversation. I felt like there was less lecturing from my point.

The therapist then shifted to reframing the problem to put it into a different perspective, one that would make their continuing to encourage Al illogical and clearly counterproductive.

In order to encourage people to depart from their customary efforts, it is no simple matter of telling them what different tack they should take. As mentioned before, people persist in what they do because they regard it as the only reasonable thing to do, the only correct thing. Simply to suggest something very different is to challenge their reality. Thus, any new tack or direction needs to be framed, packaged if you will, in an explanation that is likely to be palatable to the client. This may sound strange or artificial, but framing or reframing is part and parcel of most therapies. The difference is that in more traditional therapies, the therapist *believes* that what he is saying is "the truth," that he is "confronting the client with reality."

For example, if after only a few sessions in analysis a client says to his analyst that he now feels his problem is over and believes it's time to terminate the analysis, the analyst will frame that announcement as either a "flight into health" or some form of resistance. The analyst is in essence redefining improvement as an expected obstacle to further or "real" improvement. The analyst does not regard this reframing as creating a story, because it reflects his belief system. Whether believed or knowingly created, the reframing has the effect of inducing the analysand to remain in treatment. (Our work and that of other strategically oriented therapists has been criticized on the grounds that the outcome of a framing, however beneficial to the client, loses its legitimacy because the therapist didn't *believe* what he was saying. However, this debate goes beyond the bounds of this book.)

The therapist proceeded to present an explanation for Al's problem:

> THERAPIST: Let me say something, because I think it may put the two of you in position to help both the folks out, mainly Dad. I could see the decision to move out here as a difficult one, Dad really very much preferring not to and Mother very much wanting to. In a sense, rather than talking Dad into it there came a point where Dad was faced with this kind of choice: if I stick to my guns, I am going to make Miriam very unhappy, and I can't do that. So he acquiesced to something that he would have preferred not to do.
>
> I am assuming further that Mom also had the difficulty of seeing Dad unhappy and that what may have happened is that in knowing that he very much made the decision for her, she may have attempted to get him to be happy about it too.
>
> SARA: Hmmm!
>
> THERAPIST: And perhaps she overstated the case. She may have conveyed that while she may have her own reservations about coming here, it may be good for Dad, beneficial to him.
>
> SARA: I'm sure we were part of that too. The weather is better . . .
>
> THERAPIST: Her enthusiasm about how wonderful California is may be overblown because she is trying to convey to him that this is supposed to be useful to him. In that sense your dad is letting her down because he is not feeling very benefited.
>
> SARA AND JOHN: Yeah.
>
> THERAPIST: Since both things I have mentioned rest on the disparity between your dad's thinking "I am not that happy with California plus I am not as happy as I am supposed to be either," I think he could relax if that disparity were reduced. So that it could be conveyed to him that, one, "I'm not so sure how

happy Mama is in California, I think she tends to overstate it";
and, two, "California is a subtly difficult state to get accustomed
to." That is, "If you are having trouble getting with the apparent joie de vivre, Dad, it is a difficult change, and if you are
down, feeling depressed, feeling blue, you are entitled to that."
As a kind of message, it is the therapeutic effect of "misery loves
company," that is, "I am not alone."

Session Four

In the fourth session, the therapist again saw Sara and John.
Although they were carrying out the suggestions so far, they were
also expressing concern about taking a more clearly pessimistic position. Thus, much of this session was devoted to framing the father's
condition and their previous attempts to reassure in such a way that
they might find the therapeutic tack more acceptable.

The session ended with some specific examples of how they
might help by appearing to discourage Al from activities, rather
than encouraging him as they had been doing. Keep in mind that
we saw encouragement as the noxious agent in Al's interpersonal
milieu, and, therefore, "discouragement" was the obvious different
direction to take, peculiar as this may sound.

> THERAPIST: The common thread is that the therapeutic
> position to take is for either of you to stand in the way that he
> is taking; that is, you get in the position of holding him back. . . .
> "Should I see about my will?" "It's a lot of trouble. I would not
> do it if I were you." "Should I take the bus?" "No, I don't think
> you ought to."
>
> JOHN: (Laughs) OK.
>
> THERAPIST: "Should I go for a walk?" "It sounds like a big
> strain on you, Dad." Because to whatever extent that . . . there
> is a part of him . . . that wants to be well, that wants to get back
> in some mainstream, it needs the pressure built up. Essentially
> what you are doing is putting a dam on it and building the

pressure, and the first sign of major success is where he gets angry because you are standing in his way, and he says, "Goddammit, I'm gonna do it!"

Session Five

The treatment team felt that Miriam was still struggling with our previous attempts to get her to depart from her customary reassurances to her husband and that our efforts to frame things had not been effective. In the fifth session, therefore, we focused on a different framing: mainly that her husband's condition was caused by a lack of confidence (with which she readily agreed) and that she might help him by restoring his confidence (with which she also agreed); we suggested that one path to accomplishing that goal would be to avoid correcting his "incorrect" perceptions but, instead, to respond in a "you might be right" (i.e., nonargumentative) manner. This she also accepted.

When clients are fearful or anxious, we find it effective to offer concrete examples of how they might proceed. We do this, of course, only after they have accepted and agreed to follow the general tack we have laid out. In this particular case, we suggested that when her husband says, as he often has, "I don't know if we can make it," she could respond with "I don't know either." This response is a commiserating one and, more important, allows her to depart from her customary arguing, "Of course we will; you needn't worry."

Session Six

In the sixth session, we again saw Miriam by herself. Because we operate on the notion that the only good intervention is one that works, we usually wait to see if the client has carried out the previous suggestion, and if so, what if anything has come from it.

Miriam said that when Al voiced worries, she agreed with him rather than argued, and that it seemed to be working. For example, friends had come up from Los Angeles, and Al had enjoyed their visit.

Although Miriam reported improvement in her husband, she was still concerned about his repeated resistance to continuing treatment with his psychiatrist. When Al would express his concern about continuing with the psychiatrist, Miriam usually would reply that he still needed psychiatric care, to which he would, invariably, disagree, thus increasing her fears of his discontinuing treatment. Although we ourselves did not attach the importance she was giving to her husband's continuing treatment, we realized that she would become more anxious if he stopped. Dealing with the complainant's anxieties is, as we have emphasized, of principal importance in cases of serious problems.

Once a client has accepted a therapeutic tack, has carried it out and seen beneficial results, we need do less framing to extend her efforts into other areas of the attempted solution. Thus, in this session, we were able to provide suggestions more rapidly. Again, we framed them in a way that allowed Miriam to rejoinder to Al in a nonargumentative way: for example, when he said, "I don't think Dr. M. is doing me any good," or "I don't think I need Dr. M.," she could respond with, "I'm not sure if you need Dr. M. or if he does you any good, but it would be best to continue seeing him so as not to hurt the doctor's feelings." (In addition to departing from arguing, her statement also shifted the *reason* for continuing psychiatric treatment from a one-down position—"You're still sick; you need the doctor's help"—to a one-up position: "Stay in treatment so you can help the doctor with his feelings of self-esteem." This kind of shift can provide an additional benefit. It's the proverbial icing on the cake of commiseration.

We used an additional framing: that Al's depression stemmed from feelings of guilt that he could not express the pleasure expected of him when asked to get involved in activities such as pleasure trips and that it was this guilt that provided the main obstacle to his agreeing to try things out. Because Miriam readily agreed to this framing, we suggested that when she suggested activities or outings she should add, "I would like to do such-and-such, but I don't think you will enjoy it." In this way, we made it possible for her to depart from her customary cheerleader attempts at motivating her husband.

Session Seven

We decided to schedule the next appointment for two weeks hence and to include Sara and John. We felt that because they had also been trying to reassure Al, it would help to check back with them; at the same time, their presence in the therapy might help Miriam feel supported in her new venture with her husband.

The clients reported that Al was doing fairly well despite the fact the his psychiatrist wanted to continue seeing him for another six months. Miriam said that she had told her husband about continuing with the doctor but for the reason stated in session six, but she added that it didn't seem to have any effect. She mentioned, however, that he hadn't brought up his concerns about seeing Dr. M. since. (This is not unusual; i.e., some clients expect immediate results from some intervention, and if it is not forthcoming, they assume that what they did didn't work. When a change does occur, they might attribute it to some other influence or sometimes not notice it at all, as in this case.)

Although the family members described continuing improvement, they seemed to retain the position that Al wasn't out of the woods yet. This led to a discussion of how they would know he is. The therapist made two suggestions: one, that a sign might be Al's own determination that he is over the hump in his worries and withdrawal and, two, that it would help if they took the conservative position with him—"I'm not sure if you're up to" whatever activity they or he was suggesting—allowing Al the opportunity to say whether he was or not. This was an additional step in helping them depart from their reassurances by adopting a seemingly discouraging but not obstructing stance.

Session Eight

Miriam was seen alone in the eighth session. She reported, "Things are pretty good except for the car business." Despite considerable improvement in her husband, she still attached significance to his refusal to drive and somewhat less to his continuing to see his psychiatrist. Much of this session was spent on various options regarding the car and driving: she might suggest to him they sell the car, or tell him she had decided to take driving lessons herself so he wouldn't need to drive. We then asked to meet with her and her husband for the next session.

Session Nine

Al himself brought up the issue of their car and, later in the session, his seeing the psychiatrist. About both issues, he was rather definite: he wanted to sell the car and discontinue seeing the psychiatrist, but he added that he would find it difficult to do either because Miriam was opposed to both decisions. We framed those decisions as important ones, decisions that he needed to feel firm about.

To help him make an independent and definite decision, we turned to Miriam, asking her if she would take an oppositional position, because if she approved of his wishes, he would feel he could only have made them with her support, and he would therefore have less confidence in his own decision making. (This is an example where the therapist appears to support an action he would prefer eliminated, in this case Miriam's arguing with Al's preference, but by framing her arguing as an effort to test Al's resolve, the therapist nullifies its counterproductive effect. The reframing here is for Al's ear; thus, when Miriam expresses her customary resistance to his wishes, he will not take it as her "true" feeling but as a mechanical attempt to test his resolve.) Al responded by saying, "So, it is up to me to tell Dr. M.!"

In our clinical research project, we offer clients a maximum of ten sessions. We told Miriam and Al that they could either use that tenth session by setting another appointment or "keep it in the bank" (i.e., leave that session on an ad hoc basis). Both quickly agreed to leave it in the bank.

Follow-Up

As with all cases we see in the project, we conducted follow-up evaluations three months and one year after the last appointment. Because our model is complaint-based (as distinct from a normative or illness model), we base our judgment of the outcome on the status of the original complaint.

Thus, at the three-month follow-up we asked both Miriam and Al if they felt Al was out of the woods regarding his depression. Both said he was much better but not out of the woods completely. Miriam said he was more active and was reading and watching TV. He agreed he was not 100 percent better but was doing things, going for walks, and looking for volunteer work.

He still was not driving but said he hadn't given up the idea and hadn't sold the car. He was still seeing Dr. M. because the doctor seemed insistent on it, at least for monitoring medication. Finally, both of them said Al was no longer worried about finances and felt they had enough to live on.

In the one-year follow-up, Al said he continued to see Dr. M. about once a month for medication monitoring, but "the important thing is that I feel fine." Al's situation illustrates a problem common to people placed on a medication: it's easy to start but very difficult to know when to stop. The patient, the psychiatrist, or both are apprehensive that cessation of the medication will result in reappearance of the previous disorder. Unfortunately, the continuation of the medication serves as an implicit statement to the individual and his family that he is still "sick." It is likely that although Al and

Miriam were very relieved about his improved status, they might not regard him as out of the woods because of the implied need for further treatment.

Al had sold the car about six months before, after making a firm decision that he didn't want to drive. Al and Miriam work together volunteering in a community center. No new problems had arisen, and the couple said things were going very smoothly.

In summary, the fundamental features of this case might be stated simply:

1. The principal complainant was the wife.
2. Her complaint was her husband's depression as manifested by expressions of fearing financial ruin, threat of suicide, withdrawal from activities.
3. Her main effort to correct the situation was to reassure her husband: "Your worrying is unreasonable." In this, she was joined by her daughter and son-in-law.
4. The main therapeutic effort was to have her depart from her reassurances and, instead, adopt a position of, "Your worrying is reasonable."

The implementation of the therapeutic strategy, however, was not so simple. It had to take into account Miriam's intimidation by her husband's "severe" condition. This required our team to move carefully and slowly to make sure she would feel she was on reasonably solid ground with each step of taking a different stance with her husband. It also involved our enlisting some support from her daughter and son-in-law as well as supporting Al's treatment with Dr. M. In general, our approach illustrates the utility of recognizing a position the client is taking and incorporating it into the direction the therapist is hoping to move the client.

Al's "paranoid delusions" that his phone was being bugged and that he was being tested to see if he was insane or not were relatively mild and were expressed only to his family members. In the cases in Chapter Three, the clients' predominant symptoms were more florid delusions, the kind that can discourage therapists from working with the clients psychotherapeutically at all and certainly from contemplating brief resolution.

3

Delusions and Paranoia

When a patient expresses ideas that exceed commonly held beliefs and especially when the patient expresses them with all conviction, the problem is regarded as serious. The *serious* label is predicated on the traditional notion that such extreme expressions represent a rather fixed thought pathology; the patient's situation is all the more serious if the delusion is one of being persecuted, raising the implied threat that the patient may resort to some drastic form of retaliation or defense. In any case, the patient is considered to be beyond the reach of ordinary logic or discourse, and the therapist often feels she is dealing with someone who is deranged and possibly dangerous.

The common attempts to deal with delusions, naturally, avoid a head-on confrontation: "You think you're Jesus Christ? That's crazy!" Instead, therapists attempt to get patients to accept their delusions as invalid by *implicitly* framing them as products of mental illness. "When did you first begin to believe that . . . ?" accompanied by questions regarding stressful or exceptional events at the time of onset. Other questions may be more explicit challenges to the delusion: "When you have told other people, have you noticed they are looking strangely at you?" "Why do you think you were hospitalized? Didn't you feel something was wrong with you?" "What makes you so sure about . . . ?"

Thus, in general, traditional methods challenge the delusion, implicitly or explicitly. Most therapists assume that no productive therapy can continue until the patient acknowledges that his belief has no reasonable basis. If, in the face of the challenge, the patient persists with his delusion, the therapist usually regards the persistence as a sign of how serious the patient's condition is rather than one showing that the therapist's attempt was not a useful way of proceeding.

As with any problem, we are more interested in failed, albeit persistent, efforts to change an undesired behavior. However, in the following case examples, there are a number of common features you should keep in mind. First, these cases were all seen in private practice, and no tape recordings were made. Dialogue is therefore either summarized or a simulation of actual dialogue. Second, unlike the case in Chapter Two, in which the attempted solution is clearly delineated, in these cases it is not. The therapists were operating on assumptions, drawn from experience, of what doesn't work when trying to talk patients out of their "crazy" ideas. As we described, the traditional approach—that of attempting to challenge the patient's belief—in essence tells the patient, "Your belief is invalid. It's a product of a disordered mind."

If one is to depart from that attempted solution, the therapist's primary alternative is to take the position, "Your belief *is* valid." You will see this thread in all the case examples. This position can be hard to maintain, especially when the delusion is expressed in menacing tones and when the client implies he may take some dramatic action to protect himself from the persecution. It can help to keep in mind that trying to get the client to accept the baselessness of his belief is akin to arguing and that arguing is likely to lead to polarizing the situation.

I KNOW YOUR OFFICE IS BUGGED

This first example is from a case treated by Don Jackson (the founder and guiding spirit of the Mental Research Institute) in the early 1960s. He related it to us as an innovative way of dealing with a patient labeled as paranoid. His interventions also strongly influenced the method used in the third example in this chapter.

The patient was a married man in his early forties who had held a responsible position but was asked to take sick leave when he persisted in telling his coworkers that a governmental organization— the CIA, FBI, or some such—was keeping him under surveillance by following him, patrolling his home, and bugging his phones. At the insistence of his firm, he was to seek psychiatric care and was referred to Jackson.

Shortly after providing the usual demographic data, the patient said, in a casual manner, "I know this interview is being bugged, but let's go on anyhow." Instead of challenging that statement (e.g., "What makes you think that?" or "Have you had similar ideas in other settings?" and the like), Jackson sat upright and with an expression of marked concern and irritation said, "Goddammit, I won't allow anyone to intrude into the privacy of my work with my patients! We're not going on until we find that bug and get rid of it!" Whereupon he started looking into desk drawers, feeling under the desk, and examining his phone. The patient, still sitting, was startled by Jackson's reaction and the intensity of his search.

Jackson turned to him and said, "Don't just sit there! Help me find the damn bug! We're not going on till we find it." Jackson repeated this command, as the patient was hesitating, but finally the patient got out of the chair and made halting efforts to look under chairs, often looking to Jackson to see what he was doing. Occasionally, Jackson would ask, "Have you found it yet?" and when he got a negative reply would say, "OK; keep looking. We're not going on till we find it." After several minutes of this, the patient began to sit down, but Jackson insisted he continue to help find the bug.

Finally, the patient said, in a weary tone, "Dr. Jackson, forget the bug and the FBI. That's not what's important to me. I need to talk to you about my marriage; it's falling apart." With this, Jackson stopped his search, sat down and asked, "OK. What's the trouble in the marriage?" The session and subsequent sessions proceeded on that agenda with no further mention of the FBI or bugged phones.

What struck us about Dr. Jackson's intervention was that he avoided the customary attempted solution of challenging the delusion and instead accepted it as if it were valid. In doing so, he implicitly called attention to the patient's inconsistent behavior of sitting passively while preparing to have a private consultation with a psychiatrist whose office was bugged.

FIDEL CASTRO IS IN LOVE WITH ME

Some years later, a woman (whom we'll call Janet) was referred to me (R.F.) through the local welfare office. She was thirty-two years old, single, and unemployed. She lived on public support because she was regarded as psychiatrically disabled. When I asked her what she was coming in about, she said she didn't know how to respond to the overtures Fidel Castro was making toward her. Remembering Jackson's case and the work we had been doing in the Brief Therapy Center, I knew there was no point in challenging her notion.

> R.F.: What kind of overtures?
> JANET: Well, he's in love with me.
> R.F.: How does he let you know that? After all, he's in Cuba.
> JANET: No, he's in San Francisco.
> R.F.: Really? I'm surprised, since he's not too welcome in this country. But you never know what the government will do next. So how does he convey his love to you?

JANET: Not directly; it's always through agents of his.

R.F.: Oh; how does that go?

JANET: Well, when I'm walking down the street I'll pass by two or three men talking, and I can tell by what they're saying that it's a message from Castro that he loves me.

R.F.: Has he ever been man enough to tell you himself, directly?

JANET: No; it's always through his agents.

R.F.: Hmm. Since he loves you, has he taken you out to dinner?

JANET: No.

R.F.: Not at all? At least once?

JANET: No.

R.F.: Well, how about a lousy movie?

JANET: No; not that either.

R.F.: You mean to say this is a guy who professes his love for you but won't come right up to you and tell you himself, and he won't spend a dime on you?!

JANET: Well, I guess . . . yes, that's the case.

R.F.: Janet, you don't want to waste your time on a guy like that; you're much too good for a man like that. (*Janet smiles and looks pleased.*) Think it over, and how about if we meet again sometime next week.

JANET: (*Still smiling*) OK.

Janet started the following session saying, "You remember that stuff about Castro? Well, it's over; it's not important. Let me tell you what I really need help with. I've been out of work for a long time, and I'm tired of living on welfare. I want to get back to work, and I'm terrified of the prospect. My mind just goes blank when I start to think about it. Can you help me with that kind of problem?"

I told Janet that I worked with that kind of problem, too. The remainder of the sessions pursued that focus. She ended therapy after she had entered a job training program that also had reason-able assurance of helping her find employment.

THE MAN WHO PLEADED
I'M NOT WITH THE FBI

I (R.F.) received a phone call at my office. The caller was a minis-ter; one of his parishioners, Jerry, had sought him out that morning in a very agitated state. Jerry said he was seeking help because his work involved sensitive information, and the FBI had been keep-ing him under surveillance. The minister felt Jerry badly needed psychiatric help and asked me if I could see him as soon as possible. I told him I could see him later that morning, and we set the appointment. He said that Jerry was so anxious that he would not come alone to my office and asked whether it would be all right if he accompanied him. I said that would be fine.

Jerry was in his late twenties, was married, and had one child. When I came out to the waiting room, he and his minister were there. When I asked Jerry to come in to the office he said he wanted the minister to come with him. I readily agreed. Jerry was visibly tense and sat on the edge of the chair. I began to ask the usual iden-tifying information, but before I could get very far with it, Jerry interrupted.

> JERRY: Can you show me some identification?
>
> R.F.: Sure; what do you want to see?
>
> JERRY: How about your driver's license.
>
> R.F.: OK. (*I get up from my chair, walk over to Jerry, and open my wallet to show him the license. He takes a quick glimpse of it, and I return to my chair.*)
>
> JERRY: Thank you. That's OK.
>
> R.F.: Are you satisfied I am who I'm supposed to be: Dr. Fisch?
>
> JERRY: Yes.

R.F.: Man! You hardly looked at it; just a quick glance. You can't tell just from that. Here; take a good look at it. (*I go over to him again, showing him my license. This time, he looks at it carefully, studying the picture, glancing up at me to check it, and looking at it again.*)

Jerry: All right. It's OK.

R.F.: (*I return to my seat.*) You're satisfied now?

Jerry: Yeah, it's fine.

R.F.: God! Your minister told me on the phone that you're in a sweat about the FBI following you around, and you just accept that I'm OK from a simple driver's license?!

Jerry: Well, you've got those diplomas and your license on the wall.

R.F.: Jerry, it's nothing for the FBI to make up any kind of document. They could even outfit a whole office in no time at all. No; that won't do. I don't want you telling me anything about yourself until *I'm* convinced you're sure I'm who I'm supposed to be.

A long silence ensued as Jerry desperately looked around the office for some corroborating item. Once or twice, he looked over to his minister, apparently in hope he would get him off the hook or suggest something he himself had overlooked. However, the minister sat quietly, watching Jerry squirm. Finally, Jerry said, "Dr. Fisch, forget the FBI. That's not why I'm here. My wife is threatening to divorce me; I'm in a panic. Please, I need help with that."

The remainder of that and ensuing sessions focused on the marital problem. Jerry never brought up the FBI again. In this particular case, "going with the delusion" had an interesting effect; very quickly it reversed our original positions. At the start, Jerry was asking me to convince him of my stated identity, but I turned it around so that he was in the position of having to convince *me* of my identity.

You may note in these examples that there is a quiet playfulness in accepting the delusion rather than challenging it. You can avoid the grim struggle to get the patient to acknowledge that his notion is invalid and based on some form of psychopathology. You can instead look for the internal contradictions in the delusion. In fact, the so-called delusional patient quite often does not *act* consistently with the stated delusion.

For example, Jerry, although saying he was under constant surveillance by the FBI, never made any effort to look outside my office to see if agents were there eavesdropping, something that would have been quite consistent. In the case of the woman claiming Castro was in love with her, she didn't question how suitable he was, which would have been appropriate for a woman talking about a man who said he loved her but never paid her any attention in any tangible way.

The essence of the interventions was not so much what the therapist did but its being a *departure* from the customary attempts at dealing with the phenomenon of someone expressing an outrageous or bizarre notion. Challenging a notion can, at times, result in the individual's recanting it, but in the case of someone with paranoid delusions, challenging the delusions makes the person more firm in his or her position. This behavior does raise the question, Is persisting with a strange notion a manifestation of a fixed paranoia, or is it a response to persistent challenges to the notion? We tend to operate on the latter explanation. We have said about our work that we don't treat problems; rather, we treat attempted solutions. This approach affords a leverage in intervening that can make for rapid change, as we will see in Chapter Four, which looks at our approach to what is currently a prevalent serious problem: eating disorders.

4

Anorexia

Anorexia is regarded as a serious problem because of the imminent threat of starvation and death. That a person would persist with self-starvation to the point of jeopardizing her health, if not her life, makes this kind of problem all the more intimidating to the therapist. In addition, aside from refusing to acknowledge that there is anything wrong with her "diet," the patient has the bizarre notion that she is still too fat!

As with some other serious problems, the person in question is rarely a complainant about her own behavior; rather, the complainant is usually a parent or other close relative. All these factors set expectations for lengthy treatment. In these cases, as in all other cases, we are mainly interested in the attempts the complainants are making to bring about a change in the problem distressing them, as it is the cessation of those attempts that can bring about change in a brief period.

HENRY, SYLVIA, AND SUSAN

In the following case, the complainants were the parents. Their daughter was married and employed in their business. She was functioning quite well in her job. In all other ways, she looked and behaved in the manner customary for so-called anorectic people. She was remarkably thin and frail looking, and it was a wonder that she could maintain her job day after day. As with many anorectics, she complained that she was still overweight and that she needed to make a constant effort to prevent getting fat and ballooning out. These kinds of statements would, of course, invite her parents to argue that she was actually too thin, statements that she easily and casually discounted by saying she had all the evidence she needed when looking in the mirror. Her parents would then retreat into a silent and frustrated surrender.

Because this was a case seen in private practice, the following dialogue is a condensed simulation of the actual treatment; no taped material was available for transcript.

The initial phone call was made by Henry, the "patient's" father. He was insistent that I meet with him; his wife, Sylvia; the anorectic daughter, Susan; and two other younger daughters. The two sisters, he said, were willing to travel long distances for such a meeting because they were concerned about Susan's welfare. Although I (R.F.) prefer to limit sessions to the primary "characters" involved (in this case, it would have been the parents, as I learned on the phone that Susan was not a complainant and that the two sisters had only sporadic contact with Susan), I readily agreed to such a meeting.

Session One

Henry and Sylvia were in their early fifties, had been running a small, successful business for many years, and had employed Susan for five years in a responsible position in their firm. Susan, twenty-nine, was married and had no children. Her husband had a job unrelated to the family's business. In that first meeting, it was obvious that Susan was the center of all their concern; however, they all were making an effort to avoid labeling her as the patient.

The parents and the sisters took turns saying they were there for family therapy. Susan seemed to see through their efforts at diplomacy and rejoindered that there was nothing wrong with her and that she was sorry they all had gone to so much trouble to arrange the meeting.

HENRY: Well, Honey, you know we are concerned about you, and we feel it would be helpful if, as a family, we could understand what you're going through.

SUSAN: I'm not "going through" anything. I'm fine, and I wish you all would quit worrying about me.

SYLVIA: Susan, you're so thin; you hardly eat anything at all, and we can't help worrying about your health.

SUSAN: Oh, God!

SISTER: You know you get colds very often, sometimes the flu. You're wearing your resistance down. Can't you see that?

SUSAN: Look: I know how to take care of myself. Do you want me to look like a blimp just so you'll stop worrying?

The tenor of the session continued in that vein: the family members trying to convince Susan she was suffering from self-starvation and needed to "get some help" to change that, and Susan countering with, "There's nothing wrong with me; I simply don't want to be fat."

Session Two

Because the sisters had to return to their own localities and Susan was quite clearly not a complainant, I asked to meet with only the parents for the next session.

R.F.: Last time, I had a chance to watch you all trying to get Susan to recognize she was dangerously starving herself, but it didn't seem to get through to her. She just came back with "there's nothing wrong." Just so it might save time, would this kind of dialogue be representative of other times you've tried to help her?

HENRY: Yes. It's crazy! She's as skinny as a rail yet she insists she's overweight.

SYLVIA: Can't she see what she's doing to herself? She gets four or five colds a year; it's hard for her to find clothes that fit her, and she's always so pale. We tell her this, but she says we're making a mountain out of a molehill.

HENRY: It's terribly frustrating. She works with us every day, and she's a very hard worker; she'll often skip lunch and keep working while Sylvia and I go out.

R.F.: Do you say anything when she skips lunch?

HENRY: Of course. We plead with her to take a break. Beg her to come with us and have something to eat.

SYLVIA: She's very stubborn and insists she's not hungry and that she wants to finish the work she's doing. "You go along. Have lunch. I'm fine." Then, we'll ask her if, at least, we can bring something back for her to eat.

HENRY: Often she'll say no, she's really not hungry; but we'll bring something back anyhow. If there's any meat in the sandwich, she'll take it out, and then she'll take a bite, put it aside, and continue working. At the end of the day, most of it will still be there. It drives me nuts!

SYLVIA: When she does ask us to bring some food back, it's hardly anything. A small salad or a few crackers from the restaurant. Things like that. We'll try to bring her something more nutritious; a sandwich or something. But then, she won't even touch it.

R.F.: Folks, let me ask you something. I know you're terribly concerned about her, and you have good reason to be. But I imagine you're also puzzled. After all, she's an intelligent woman and quite capable. You said she's been a distinct asset in the business. I'd like to ask you what's your best guess why she is doing this to herself?

This question attempted to elicit the parents' frame of reference about Susan and her problem—their position.

HENRY: I know this may sound crazy, but Susan has always prided herself on facing challenges and without help; it has always seemed important that she could tackle things single-handedly. She's very competitive. Her sisters have struggled to keep their weights down, and as you might tell, they haven't done too well with it. I wouldn't be surprised if she's bound and determined to show them what she can do. But that's just a guess.

This formulation is what makes sense to Henry, possibly Sylvia. What follows is a way of using his reality to aid them in shifting away from "Please, you must eat more." The logical alternative is the position, "You shouldn't eat so much."

In a number of cases, clients are prepared to shift when they realize that what they've been doing simply doesn't work. But with serious problems, it takes more than the clients' simply realizing their tack doesn't work, because the clients are intimidated by the patient's condition and the fearful risk if they err in dealing with it. Thus, working with what makes sense to them but reframing it can help them get around their paralyzing intimidation.

In the dialogue that follows, we have put deliberately selected wording in boldface type to make clear that successfully enlisting the clients' motivation is not only a matter of conveying a thought but of *how* the thought is expressed.

R.F.: (*Continuing from previous dialogue*) Well, it's just a guess, but I can see the sense in it. So I wouldn't throw the idea out too quickly. If that's the kind of thing which motivates her, would that mean that she wouldn't be attracted to an effort in which she was getting help?

HENRY: Probably not. She's extremely independent. (*Sylvia is nodding in agreement.*)

R.F.: Is it **possible** that that might explain why your best efforts to get her to eat have backfired? That you were inadvertently feeding into her prime motivation, to do things in the face of challenge?

When you attempt to get a client to consider a new and novel premise, your asking if it's *possible* enhances the effort, because clients will grant most things are *possible*. You can then continue as if the premise is *likely*.

> HENRY: Yes; that makes a lot of sense. But what else could we do? We can't just stand by and watch her deteriorate.
>
> R.F.: No, of course not. But it's not a choice between continuing an effort that doesn't work or doing nothing. It's a matter of learning from experience to do something that *will* work. Over and over, you have learned that trying to help her eat more has **backfired**. Does that give you any ideas?

Backfired is more confirmatory than *doesn't work*. *Doesn't work* can leave the impression that the clients' efforts are simply ineffective, whereas *backfired* implies that they are counterproductive, detrimental. We also see here that I moved slowly by asking if what I said gave them any ideas. The clients are more likely to accept a new tack if they suggest the direction rather than feel that the therapist is pushing the idea.

> SYLVIA: You mean we should stop urging her to eat?
>
> R.F.: I'm not sure that just stopping it will help. It runs too high a risk that she'll just interpret your silence as a temporary lull in your usual efforts; she's likely to be waiting for you to say the kind of thing you've said before. No, I think it has to be something that conveys you've changed your song.
>
> HENRY: Well, I guess it would have to be something like *discouraging* her from eating.
>
> R.F.: Yes, I think so. . . . Would this be **feasible**? When the two of you are preparing to go out to lunch, ask her if she wouldn't mind working over the lunch period. You don't offer to bring her anything back. If she asks, and only if she asks for it, you say, "Sure." Except, when you get back you realize you'd forgotten, and you're terribly apologetic. "Can you wait till dinnertime?"

SYLVIA: That's just the opposite of what we do! *(Laughs)*

HENRY: What if she gets angry that we forgot to bring her anything?

R.F.: Has she ever gotten angry that you weren't pushing the food? *(They both shake their heads.)* Then, if she does, you'll know you're on the right track.

Look, I know this must still seem strange to you despite your past experiences with her. **I'm not asking you to rush into it.** It would be better if you thought it over carefully **before you try it out.** And because you don't know what her reaction would be, it would be best to consider it an **experiment.**

We prefer to make the error of moving too slowly rather than too quickly. Here, I formulated a tangible suggestion, one based on the clients' frame of reference and whose direction was given by the clients. However, in serious cases, we keep in mind that the client is likely to be skittish about doing anything different for fear of making a dangerous misstep. Therefore, we prefer to convey, "Take your time."

I followed up with what appeared to be an echoing of that idea—"think it over carefully"—but then added a qualifier which implied that after thinking it over, they would do it (our appreciation to Milton Erickson for this kind of "suggestion").

Finally, to further allay their apprehension about trying something very different, I urged them to label the new tack as an experiment. An experiment permits curiosity in the experimenter, and curiosity tends to displace anxiety. The experiment label also implies that the new tack can be discarded if the experiment doesn't work; it can be done and undone as needed.

Session Three

The third session was held two weeks later.

R.F.: I know I made a suggestion last time and asked you to give it some thought, so **I'm interested in your thinking** about it.

Note that I did not ask them if they *did* it. If I had, and they said they hadn't done it, it would place them and me in an awkward position. But asking what their thinking was allowed them to state their acceptance or rejection of the idea and give their reasons. This phrasing, then, allowed me to take an accepting position of their thinking. As it turned out, this carefulness was not necessary, but, as we've said before, it's better to take things too slowly than too quickly.

HENRY: Well, we did it! As we were leaving for lunch one day last week, I asked Susan if she wouldn't mind staying over lunchtime to finish up some work that needed doing. She said that would be all right, but could we bring her back a sandwich or a light salad, and we said, "Sure."

When we got back, empty-handed, she asked where her lunch was. I said, "Oh, God. I'm terribly sorry, Honey. I clean forgot." I didn't offer to go out and get her something, but I must confess I was tempted to. She didn't get angry, but she looked disappointed, and the rest of the day went uneventfully.

SYLVIA: The next day really was a surprise. We thought it would go as usual. However, at the lunch break Susan asked us if she could come with us to lunch! (*Henry is grinning.*)

HENRY: It may sound like a small thing, but she's never asked before. We'll always ask her if she wants to join us, and she always refuses. And, at lunch, she said she was hungry. She's never said that before either, and this time, she didn't pick at her food. Ate the whole sandwich!

Henry and Sylvia were obviously pleased about the outcome of the "experiment." It is tempting, under these circumstances, for the therapist to congratulate the clients for what they have done and to suggest they push their new approach further. Keeping in mind that the effectiveness of the therapy depends on the clients' *departure* from their previous tack, any initial success perceived by them as a significant change, albeit small, helps them stay with that new effort and avoid going back to what is confirmed as a counterproductive thrust.

As a general rule, when clients report what sounds like improvement, we ask if it is a change in the problem before making any confirmation of their success. If, as is sometimes the case, the clients say they don't regard it as any meaningful change, we know not to congratulate them but instead simply to nod. At times, we might ask what a significant change would look or sound like. This can give useful information about where to focus any further inquiry and interventions.

Sessions Four and Five

I saw Henry and Sylvia twice more, each session separated by two and three weeks. They reported that Susan was now regularly taking her lunchtimes, usually joining them. They had also noticed that her choice of food was expanding, as was her appetite, and her appearance was beginning to reflect these changes. They and I agreed not to schedule any more appointments but to leave them on an as-needed basis.

In this case, there were a number of favorable factors that we believe made the task of persuasion easier. First, the clients' daughter was an adult, not an adolescent. Second, she had established herself as capable of sound judgment, at least in their eyes. She worked steadily and productively, and they regarded her as a reliable asset in their business. She was married, and the marriage was stable.

As we have said previously, the tactical challenge when attempting to intervene in serious problems does not so much concern the nature of the complaint nor the identification of the complainants' problem-maintaining efforts. Rather, the difficulty lies in getting the complainants to accept a departure from those efforts. (With few exceptions, the customary attempt is to urge the anorectic to eat more.) We have often been frustrated to see clearly what needs to be done and then to find that we have failed in motivating the client to follow up on a suggestion.

For example, in another case, the anorectic had been in the care of an internist, and although his efforts had not produced any change, the parents trusted him. However, we failed to contact him. In hindsight, it might have made a strategic difference if we had spoken with him and had enlisted his support in our efforts.

In other cases of anorexia, as well as in other serious cases, we have, usually unwittingly, taken too optimistic a stance and left the family with the impression we weren't taking their child's condition seriously enough; in cases like these, the parents are viewing their child as a sick, helpless victim of some strange inner psychological quirk. The parents also are intimidated by the strangeness of the "disease." As we have said before, there is less likelihood of error in moving too slowly than too quickly, because the parents are extremely uneasy about "doing something wrong." In other cases, we have moved too fast, attempting to get the family members to change their efforts before they had time to become committed to the potential benefit.

———

In the following case, there are a number of similarities to the case of Henry, Sylvia, and Susan. The anorectic was a married adult; she had been able to pursue a career until she became too ill. We include this case because of a striking feature. In the first session, because of the therapist's slow and painstakingly thorough method of eliciting the basic elements of the problem and, more important, the parents' attempted solution, the futility of those efforts became so clear to the parents that they shifted to a different tack on their own. The therapist did not need to make any further efforts to persuade them to depart from what they had been doing.

This case was treated by John Weakland (J.W.) in the Brief Therapy Center. We are therefore able to present actual dialogue.

We include a goodly portion of the dialogue from the first session so that you can see how J.W. brought out relevant data so clearly that the case turned around much faster than we would have anticipated; only three sessions were required.

It is ironic that we have developed an approach to doing therapy briefly and have devoted more than thirty years to refining and using it, yet at times are surprised how quickly some cases improve. Some years before, rather early in the Center's development, we were reviewing "failure cases," which included clients who dropped out of therapy. One client had failed to return for her third appointment, and we had classified her as a dropout. But when we played the tape of the second session, we all heard her say, clearly and emphatically, that what she had gotten out of treatment far exceeded her expectations; she was no longer bogged down by her problem (depression), and she detailed specific actions she was taking that echoed her dramatic improvement. We stopped the tape in utter befuddlement. All of us—her therapist and five observers—had been present during this session, yet *none* of us could remember her saying these things, and, as we continued the tape, we heard the therapist say, "OK, I'll see you again next week"! We could only assume that we were deaf to her comments because we were still hung up on the psychoanalytic concept of flight into health—that her report of improvement was not real and was therefore to be discounted. Such is the power of one's frame of reference.

DAUGHTER DOESN'T EAT
AND DAD'S A NERVOUS WRECK

We had been contacted by Jack and Peggy, the parents of a thirty-one-year-old married daughter, Janice, who we were told had anorexia. Unlike Susan in the previous case, she had recently been hospitalized. We met with only the parents, not only for the first session but also for the remainder of the therapy. We never met their daughter. This may seem strange to readers who are more comfortable with traditional family therapy, whose model assumes that symptomatic behavior by any one member of the family represents an underlying "dysfunctional homeostasis" of the entire family.

If one proceeds according to that model, it would logically follow that in order to relieve the symptomatic behavior, the family's communicational functioning would have to be fundamentally revised, in which case *all* members should participate in the therapy. Our model, although still encompassing an interactional view, is different. That is, we view the symptomatic behavior as something primarily *maintained* by the very efforts the complainants are making to resolve that behavior; their efforts create, in effect, a positive feedback loop—a vicious cycle. Thus, a departure from the repetitive efforts of *any* member of the loop can reverse the feedback loop, thereby eliminating the problem-maintaining efforts.

Session One

J.W. began the case with our customary question.

> J.W.: What's the problem?
>
> PEGGY: It's our daughter. She's thirty-one, and she's not eating. She had an eating problem when she was twelve, but it disappeared shortly after. It resurfaced in high school. She would complain about stomach pain. Now, she's married . . . for five years . . . and has a child, three and a half years old. She also has a lot of pressure in her job.
>
> J.W.: Is she still in the hospital?
>
> PEGGY: No. She was in the hospital only for three weeks, but they wouldn't let her out without her promising to come to their clinic two or three times a week. . . . She's very tiny, less than five feet, and she's in her seventies [pounds]. . . . We're hoping you can help us cope with this situation.

Throughout her narration, Jack sat tensely, his hands folded to his face in a prayer-like fashion, his head bent, looking down, giving the impression of a listener who is anxiously waiting for his turn to say something of importance. Peggy, in contrast, was much more collected, and her comments were clear and well organized in their delivery. She appeared to be the cool head yet conveyed that she too felt it was a desperate situation.

PEGGY: *(Continuing)* It's been suggested she may have candida. She gets nauseated as soon as she eats. She's fearful of throwing up. She's said she'd rather not eat than risk throwing up. I've said to her, "What's wrong with throwing up?" but she's still afraid of it. . . . We're falling apart, and [Jack's] very upset. It's weighing heavily on us.

J.W.: It seems that whatever Janice is doing it's not effective. *(Both nod.)* Tell me more about it weighing heavily.

PEGGY: We get these phone calls from her, telling us how badly she feels. They're very discouraging. I almost don't want to talk to her.

JACK: Yes. It's very upsetting to hear her talking about her condition, her stomach pains, her not eating.

PEGGY: And he'd be at me *(Referring to Jack)* after a visit to the hospital. *(Paraphrasing)* "What are we going to do!?"

You may be able to sense the near terror these people were feeling: Jack, barely able to control his panic and sense of helplessness; Peggy, holding herself together in an effort to maintain some stability for the both of them.

PEGGY: She expresses a desire to eat. . . . She feels it's something physical . . . but it could be emotional too. She's said it was very difficult to grow up in our household.

JACK: *(Elaborating on that idea)* I used to work [in a hazardous setting]. . . . That was bad enough, but I'd bring the damned work home with me. . . .

J.W.: It must be exhausting for you *(To Peggy)*. The trips to the hospital; taking care of the baby . . .

PEGGY: *(Weakly and sadly)* Yes.

They began to detail the medical care Janice had received, partly to inform J.W. but also partly to justify their frustration and desperation.

JACK: At XYZ Hospital [a different one], the doctor had a closed mind! Janice had asked him about candida. "Where'd you get that idea?" He told her, point blank, "I don't believe in it!" He just cut her off! (*Jack's speech, at this point, is very rapid and pressured.*) OK, if you believe that, all right. But there are more diplomatic ways of putting it. . . . Don't tell her that to her face! [Jack went on to say that in consulting a second doctor at that hospital, the same thing happened, increasing their frustration.]

J.W.: There seem to be three sides to this very difficult situation . . . and it sounds as if she's not getting competent or useful medical attention.

By "three sides," J.W. was referring to the speculations about the candida infestation, the "emotional" factors, and the unidentified and vague "physical" factors. However, the main purpose of this comment was to establish that J.W. recognized their sense of helplessness, of feeling lost and scared.

JACK: Correct! Correct!

PEGGY: She's seen a number of doctors, and now she's seeing a holistic one, so we're hoping that this time . . .

J.W.: It'd be better to keep your fingers crossed. The safest course is not to build your hopes up to a possible letdown.

This comment also echoed his commiserating with their position. The important point here is that in the face of such clear-cut pessimism on the parents' part, J.W. wanted to avoid taking an optimistic stance, certainly not an explicit one.

PEGGY: (*Nodding*) Be realistic; yes.

J.W.: (*Now turning to Jack*) What's your main concern?

JACK: That she eats! . . . Unless she puts weight on, she dies. I don't want that to happen. . . . (*Jack is understating his emotions to give more emphasis to the seriousness of his concerns. However, it seems as if he's unable to maintain that feigned calmness, and he continues.*) I'm considering talking to her, to appeal to her to eat if not for her own sake then for the sake of her child, that cute little boy who needs her (*Starting to cry*) . . . but I'm not sure whether to address that or not.

J.W.: Well, at this early stage I'm not sure what to advise, but as a general rule it's better to take your time, not force an answer on her. . . . Don't push it; the fact that you're uncertain means that you're not clear and that there are a number of complex factors.

Without asking directly, J.W. could safely assume from what had already been said that Jack had attempted to help Janice by urging, exhorting her to eat and that he was considering pushing ahead with yet another salvo of more of the same. Having framed the problem as discouraging in its complexity, the therapist was advising Jack to "go slow" and thereby back away from his campaign of "EAT! EAT!"

JACK: Yeah, yeah. . . . [But he lapses back into agitated desperation thinking of the catastrophic impact on their grandchild should Janice starve to death.] You see mothers who would do anything for their child; I sometimes wonder if Janice cares enough; if she lacks enough feeling for the little guy, enough bonding.

J.W. then shifted to asking about their attempts at solving the problem. This is highly important information, of course: in our model, it is the keystone in maintaining a problem.

J.W.: It would be helpful for me to know how you've been trying to help Janice; trying to help in any sort of way.

PEGGY: We've had serious talks, about her growing up.

J.W.: What would those talks be like?

Clients frequently give information by using shorthand, giving a brief summary statement or just a label. But the absence of specific dialogue obscures the message being sent, leaving only the *intent* of the message. This is part of the complexity of human verbal communication: it's not only that the message sent is not necessarily the message received but also that the message intended is not necessarily the message sent. Thus, the therapist often has to ask for the message itself, the verbatim dialogue. (In this case, we are not including the parents' reply.)

J.W.: What other sorts of things have you done to better her situation?

PEGGY: Fix food for her. But then she'll say, "Oh, I can't eat that," and I'll ask her, "What can you eat?" She'll only eat vegetables, but when I've fixed that she won't eat it. . . . (*Leaning forward*) You know, it's like someone diving out of an airplane. I don't know how to give her that push.

J.W.: How have you tried?

PEGGY: By offering her food—things I think she'd like. Sometimes she'll say, "I wish I could eat that, eat everything," and I'd tell her, "I wish you could too, and I think you will." Beyond that, I don't know how to persuade her.

What I'd really like to know is, should we let her know how we feel. Inside, I fall apart, but in front of her I keep a stiff upper lip. He [Jack] is more likely to show it. He's hovering over her— "Do you like this? Do you want this?" With that nervousness, she just tightens up.

J.W.: Anything else?

PEGGY: To help her? I've thought it would be better to just help her relax, not to make a thing out of food; perhaps letting her *ask* for it rather than offering it to her. You might say ignoring it. I've started to do that this past weekend.

JACK: *(Expressing his frustration in trying to help)* . . . How can you help!? How the hell can I get inside her!?

J.W.: *(Still pursuing the attempted solution)* How have you tried?

JACK: By being close to her, pushing her. If she eats a little bit of food, I encourage. She'll say, "I don't want you to encourage me." But I'll tell her, "You're pleasing me, and right now that's all that counts."

J.W.: You're urging her, encouraging her, "Eat it, eat it!"?

JACK: That's what I'm trying to do; trying to get her to eat. It's tunnel vision, all I can see. "Eat, eat, eat!"

J.W., after a phone call from the observers on the team, asked about the matter of the candida, specifically whether and how it could be confirmed. Jack said that the current doctor said it could be found in a stool sample; he has sent one to a laboratory back east, but it would take two weeks to find out the results. J.W. then concluded the session with a different agenda.

J.W.: Before we stop today, I'd like you to think about a first sign of improvement. I say a "first sign" because it's a very serious situation with your daughter, and she's got a long way to go. Therefore, it's important to think about a signpost along the way. What first thing which would be observable? Think small and concretely.

This was delivered as a piece of homework for the parents to consider before the next session. Such a task can elicit useful information (e.g., clarifying how a client defines a change), but it is, at the same time, a form of intervention. Implied in the question is the premise that things can change, can improve. By addressing the question, the client is accepting the premise and thus operating with a sense of hopefulness. This is all the more useful when the clients, as in this case, are seeing only hopelessness. This "therapeutic optimism" can, in turn, allow clients to relax a bit and release the grip on their desperate attempts to solve the problem.

Session Two

Peggy and Jack came back a week later. The original therapist, John Weakland, was away, and I (R.F.) conducted this session. Because I had directly observed the previous session, my substitution was a simple matter. The session began with my explaining this idea to Jack and Peggy, who readily accepted it.

We had noted that in the first session, little was asked about Janice's husband—what role, if any, he played in the problem, and his concern about it. Because it is very important to us to determine who the complainants are in a problem, I brought up Janice's husband in this session.

> R.F.: Where does her husband fit in in all of this, especially since he lives with her?
>
> PEGGY: His attitude is that Janice is fine. It's not that he's not concerned; he is. It's that he's not that sophisticated, doesn't understand how critical it is. To him it's just something that is passing.
>
> R.F.: Are you saying that he's not alarmed—
>
> JACK: (Interrupting) He doesn't seem to be that alarmed. He doesn't understand . . . he doesn't know what could happen.
>
> PEGGY: . . . Janice will be fine; she'll be good.
>
> R.F.: Is his casual approach a problem for either of you?

They both said it wasn't. Their description of his attitude toward Janice's condition made it likely that he wasn't a complainant. He was not expressing distress about it, and because to him it was a "passing thing," it was doubtful he would feel expert intervention was necessary. If the situation had been otherwise, we would probably have asked him to come in. Jack then shifted to a different focus.

> JACK: I'm like a mirror, not good at masking my feelings. [Peggy's] good at it. So I've found the best thing is to keep away from her and let her handle it . . . and it's working. And he [Janice's husband] is able to be calm, and he's doing her more good than harm.
>
> R.F.: If I hear you right, his being more laid back is helping her.

In addition to clarifying Jack's statements, this comment also reinforced the benefits of departing from their attempted solution of pressuring Janice to eat.

> R.F.: This is a slight digression (*To Jack*), but you said since you're too intense and nervous, you've been inclined to stay away and let Peggy handle things. . . . So I don't know what that meant. Like what kind of contact have you been having with her?
>
> JACK: When she's visiting us, I'll keep out of the kitchen or dining room. Asking her, "How do you feel? Are you eating enough today?" I don't ask that anymore; just give her a hug and fade out of the room or go to the store. I try to avoid verbal contact. . . . If I start weaving toward that [pressuring Janice] Peggy gives me a signal. It makes sense because it's paying off. . . . It looks good so far.
>
> R.F.: . . . and paying off measured by how?

Asking for specifics can accomplish several things. First, the report becomes clearer, moving from the vague to the definite. Second, you get an idea of how the client measures change, of his or her priorities. Third, by reporting the specifics of a change to you, the client sees the change as more real, more meaningful.

> JACK: The fact that she's eating a little bit.
>
> PEGGY: She's eating more—

JACK: *(Interrupting)* She's eating more. . . . She's eating more solid food.

R.F.: Since when, by the way?

We ask this question because sometimes, in the first session, the clients may not have made clear that some improvement had already occurred before they consulted a therapist. Or the timing of improvement may reflect some impact from that first session. It is always important to know if this is the case, because you need to highlight any definable improvement; it also allows you to find out what in particular made for that improvement.

PEGGY: Since this past week . . . Sunday, I made breakfast— cinnamon toast, poached eggs. She ate pretty good. She's starting to eat a little bit more. By the end of the week, she didn't need to use the hot water bottle anymore. *(Peggy had earlier mentioned that Janice complained of abdominal pain after almost every meal; she would use a hot water bottle to relieve it.)* She's still conscientious about what she eats, writing down the caloric intake.

R.F.: Well, that doesn't surprise me, because her condition is such a serious one, a discouraging one. That's one of the reasons I didn't even think of asking if there had been any change in a week's time. But I'm surprised. She's certainly not out of the woods by any means, but you're saying she's eating more, not using the hot water bottle. I can't attribute the improvement to anything we've done here. All we did was ask questions.

There are several implications embedded in this response to Peggy's statement that Janice is still watching her caloric intake. I was less likely to err if I assumed the parents were still in a pessimistic position, still fearful about Janice's shaky condition. I echoed their position, thus making any further comments more credible. I then used that "pessimism" to explain that I was surprised by the rapidity of improvement; I didn't even think to ask. However, I nonetheless established that a desirable change had occurred, and faster than I had anticipated. Thus, starting from "She's not out of the woods," I was talking about improvement. Finally, by disavowing any credit for the change, I was implying that *they* had done something, that they were not helpless bystanders.

JACK: Well, it took the pressure off my mind, started me thinking. . . . He [John Weakland] took a lot of pressure off me. I couldn't think . . . don't ask me why . . . I was directed into the right channel.

PEGGY: That session was very helpful.

R.F.: Really? You know, when you're very focused on what you're doing, you don't know how you're coming across. So, I'm curious about two things, and let me take them one at a time. What was said that—

JACK: I can't put my finger on it . . .

PEGGY: It was something we desperately needed. The situation with him (*Pointing to Jack*) was dreadful, out of control . . . every minute of the day. And after being here and speaking with Dr. Weakland . . . the questions he asked . . .

R.F.: Which leads to the second question. Again, you may not be able to put your finger on it. . . . Are you aware of what you've done differently this week that would have been different from previous times?

PEGGY: We went to her home where it's quiet, peaceful, tranquil—nobody asking questions, no pressure. No more rushing her. Helped her relax. It was like a vacation for me . . . because Jack, God bless him, it's that nervousness, tension just bouncing off the walls.

R.F.: You mean it's like Ed Sullivan? He could brighten a room just by leaving it. (*Jack and Peggy laugh.*)

PEGGY: In this case, he tranquilized it by leaving.

Although humor should be used carefully, it can be beneficial for clients. It brings the intensity of the problem down from the pathological to a familiar *human* context; it helps by normalizing a problem and therefore implies a less mysterious, more changeable state of affairs. People tend to be more open to new ideas when they are relaxed.

> R.F.: *(To Jack)* Since you felt more relaxed after the session with Weakland, if in visiting Janice . . . if you—
>
> JACK: I didn't go over there at all. The pressure was off her. *(Pointing to Peggy)* I stayed home.
>
> R.F.: So you helped out but not in a way that was flattering?

This comment, on the surface, could be taken as belittling Jack's role. But I was more interested in the supportive implications of it: that what he *did* was strategically useful to Janice but that I would understand he might not get the credit he deserved. If he interpreted my comment otherwise, I would have clarified my intent. As it turned out, he was not at all discomforted by it. Jack cheerfully said, "When I met her today, her face, her attitude was entirely different. She had the vitality she didn't have last week. She was laughing."

Throughout the remainder of the session, Peggy and Jack reiterated how valuable the first session was to them. Their comments on their attempted solution were always put in the past tense: "Before, we would . . . " Their statements about Janice's improvement were qualified, however, as we saw earlier, leaving open the question of whether they felt the need for more help or not. On the one hand, we do not want to suggest termination when the client is not feeling ready for it; on the other hand, we do not want to prolong therapy the client doesn't feel is necessary. The latter position can have a discouraging influence; it can, unwittingly, convey that what has been accomplished is not enough, is trivial. Jack and Peggy's report of the change in Janice was, for us, a significant and qualitative improvement. But we are more interested in whether the clients view the change as significant and, if so, to what degree. I brought up this consideration.

R.F.: Since you both have said you feel more settled down after that session with Weakland, I don't know if you've achieved what you had hoped to. After all, it's only one session. Or do you feel you're not out of the woods yet?

PEGGY: She can have a setback any time, and she's still not taking in enough calories . . . a scary thing for her. I have to calm her down. She can't be gaining weight, but she's taking in solid food now. She used to be on liquids. This is the right tack even if it's a thimbleful each day.

R.F.: So if we were to ask to see you again, you wouldn't feel it would be wasting your time?

JACK: At this stage, I don't know. I don't want to cut something off if it will help her out.

PEGGY: Do you think it [more sessions] is necessary?

Here I suggested two options. They could stop now, leaving the remainder of the ten sessions in the bank should they later feel the need to return, or they could continue until they felt more sure about terminating. Because they continued to equivocate, I said, "Let me suggest a compromise between the two. I know John will be back next week. I'd like to ask the two of you to come back."

What you say and how you put it should always take the position of the clients into consideration. In this case, the clients' stated position was ambiguous, neither strongly optimistic nor pessimistic. In such a case, there is less chance of error in taking the pessimistic position. If you are wrong, and it turns out that you underestimated the clients' optimism, the clients are likely to correct your impression. But if you err the other way, underestimating the clients' pessimism, you run the risk of their feeling you don't understand the seriousness of the situation, that you are trivializing it. Thus, in the face of Jack and Peggy's equivocation, I suggested they come back even if it was just once more. As it turned out, they were more relaxed about the problem than it had appeared:

PEGGY: What about coming in a couple of weeks? Is that possible?

JACK: Yes, then we'd have more to report on.

R.F.: OK. Why don't we set it up for two weeks.

Session Three

As it turned out, the third and last session took place three weeks later, again with John Weakland.

> J.W.: It's been three weeks since you met with Dr. Fisch, and at that time things had improved so much that to tell you the truth it made me a little nervous, so I'm wondering what has happened in the three weeks since.

This framing, which we might call being nervous about rapidity of improvement, allows the clients to relax regardless of what they have to report. For example, if on the one hand they say things are unchanged since the last visit or even have worsened, you can appear to breathe a sigh of relief, which eliminates their concern that they are being chastised for not doing better. On the other hand, if things have continued to improve, this good news easily offsets any concern about your "nervousness." After all, the clients live with the problem.

> PEGGY: It's been progress. Little bits of steady progress. Janice has made progress. She is consuming food, she hasn't put on any weight 'cause her diet is so limited. She has been diagnosed with having the worst case you can have of candida. Which means she can eat no sugars, yeasts, molds, which includes all breads, pastas, and anything fattening; so she is eating vegetables, chicken, fish. She is not likely to put on any weight, but I kept telling her, "At least you are on the right road; you are consuming foods, not just liquids."

J.W.: From what I remember you told me before, even if the most one could say was that things had stabilized, it would still be a positive step, and she is eating in the limited range without struggle or urging.

PEGGY: Right. There is no urging. She has a lot of discomfort after she eats. Even that is not every day. She would eat a little bit before, and she would have to have a hot water bottle 'cause she had so much pain. Now, the hot water bottle is maybe once or twice a week. She is continuing to see different doctors who may help her. That has been very expensive, but it has helped too.

J.W.: Is she having any better success at finding understanding and useful doctors than what you told me about the first time?

PEGGY: Yes. She found one that diagnosed the candida. He was very understanding but was very vague, and she wants something more tangible.

JACK: She has now found a doctor that has deeper knowledge of this disease.

J.W.: It is very difficult to find just one person who is just right in almost anything.

PEGGY: She has a lot of allergies to food, which makes it very difficult for her to eat. Although she is doing better, I am still kind of leery. If there is something that turns her around and she starts getting depressed again.

J.W.: Let me say first that I think it's much more sensible to remain kind of leery after the history of seriousness of things than it would be to sort of wave a banner and say, "Hurrah! Hurrah! It is all settled." That would not be very realistic. You are on the safer side to retain a certain cautious skepticism until things proceed further.

PEGGY: That's what I'm doing.

J.W.: Good.

Again, J.W. maintained credibility by echoing the clients' pessimism but stepped from there to the optimistic *implication* that things can or are likely to "proceed further," to get better. This is similar, in principle, to the use of implication in hypnosis: "You will start to feel a lightness in your hand *before it begins to lift*." This position is in marked contrast to traditional therapy, in which the client's pessimism would be regarded as discouraging, just pessimistic. In that situation, the therapist would be inclined to try to talk the client out of her pessimism: "Look on the brighter, more hopeful side!"

JACK: I have also been encouraging her to see a good nutritionist. I have set her up with two different ones in the area. She will have to choose.

J.W.: I certainly hope that that is useful to her, but as I remember, from your interview with Dr. Fisch, if I have it correct, and let me know if I haven't, the direction you were moving in at that time was to be watchful but to back off or cut down on how you were actively involved in her situation and leave it a bit more up to her?

PEGGY: Yes.

JACK: She's going to eventually have to handle her own life, so it was a good way of getting out of it.

J.W.: So, unless you have seen something that would change your mind, in general it would be best to sort of keep on that same tack.

PEGGY: At the present time I'm still staying with her, over where she lives. I help her shop and kind of be there and support her. Little by little, I see her doing more.

J.W.: OK. I am not speaking about the pace at which you back off a little and leave things more up to her, because I cannot judge that from a distance. Just sort of the general direction of your policy.

JACK: That has been the general direction, and we have done it slowly rather than putting everything on her lap and saying, "Here it is. It is all yours."

PEGGY: And as she feels better, she is making comments which I consider great. "If I continue to feel this good, I will be able to drive myself to the appointments with Dr. so and so." She is thinking along those lines.

J.W.: That is encouraging, but again that is partly a matter of not having it happen too fast or to get up undue expectations even. I think the best thing you might tell her in a situation like that is, "Well, it sounds good, but don't push yourself on that. It may take a little longer than you are expecting." Otherwise, if she got unrealistic about the expectations or the pace of her improvement—

JACK: She has told me that her expectation is that this is going to take around one year, and we are only two or three months into it.

J.W.: Well, that's good. What I am saying is for you to go along with that rather than attempt to encourage things beyond a pace at which it really can develop.

JACK: Basically, we are letting her set the pace, and we are following, encouraging her all the way.

J.W.: Hmm; but that is exactly what I mean. Encouraging her all the way. Are you encouraging her or pushing her a little bit more than might be useful?

JACK: I don't do any pushing. I stay clear and do that by staying away, keeping out of her hair and leaving her alone.

J.W.: OK. How are you encouraging her, then?

JACK: For example, when we talk on the phone, I don't ask her, "How do you feel?" That is the worst question I can ask.

J.W.: Good!

JACK: What I'll say when I see her is "You look really good today. You seem active and everything." And she says, "You know, some other people have told me that too." So she knows I'm being honest about it, and she responds to my comments with a smile, whereas before she would growl at me and dismiss me.

J.W.: As long as she smiles at that, fine, but if you see her look skeptical. . . . It is not safe to count on a steady improvement but rather two steps forward and one step back, as many changes occur. There is still the possibility that one day you will be there and you say the same as usual, and she will indicate she does not believe that. So I am proposing that you keep your eyes open for that possibility, and if it does come up, you take that as a signal, and you back away because you are going beyond what she is prepared for, at least for that day, anyway.

JACK: I watch her before I say anything. I put my mind in gear before I open my mouth.

J.W.: That's good, but it's a tough job!

Near the end of this last session, J.W. asked if they had any other concerns about Janice. Both said no, that it was only her eating and the effects it had been having on her health and spirit. They reiterated that they felt they understood the more effective path to take and that they were encouraged by the results so far. J.W. then suggested that they stop therapy now but with the option of reopening at any time they felt it might be necessary. They readily agreed to keeping the remaining sessions in the bank.

Follow-Up

As is customary in the Brief Therapy Center, we conducted a follow-up telephone interview with both Jack and Peggy, the first about six months after their last session. Each said they felt less concerned about Janice's condition, that she was showing slow but gradual progress. Peggy cited as an example that Janice was now getting dressed instead of sitting in her robe all day. She added that Janice was planning to return to work the following week.

We conducted the second follow-up approximately one year after the last session. As for their concern about Janice, Jack said, "Less, much less." He reported that Janice's hair was coming back, that she was working out of her home, driving her car, and eating regularly. The pains she experienced in her stomach were now less frequent, and Peggy felt much less need to help Janice out. Peggy echoed that report. "She's more on her own feet."

In reviewing this case, it would seem that the main therapeutic impact was made in the first session. At that time, the questioning we routinely do to elicit a clear statement of the problem and, accordingly, a clear picture of the attempted solution had an unexpectedly strategic effect. The discussion highlighted, clearly enough, that urging Janice to eat was, at the very least, nonproductive, and possibly making matters worse. It was unclear how much the clients understood that, but however limited their understanding, they put it into effect in their own fashion, and their restraining themselves from pushing had a beneficial and durable effect.

As we discussed earlier, "anorectic" behavior is intimidating to attempt to resolve, in great part because of its health- or life-threatening aspects. In the next chapter, we take up a different form of such threat, one more common than anorexia—namely, the problem of excessive drinking. Unlike anorexia, whose impact rarely goes beyond the family, excessive drinking can have more widespread consequences to the population at large. Drunk driving is one of the most dramatic examples, along with the contribution excessive drinking makes to crimes of violence. We felt that the subject of excessive drinking clearly deserved to be included in a work dealing with intimidating problems.

5

Alcoholism

The labels *alcoholism* and *alcoholic,* both emotionally laden terms, represent a viewpoint significantly different from ours. More consistent with our viewpoint would be *undesired drinking* or, more accurately, *complained-about drinking.* Because of the emotionalism associated with the problem of alcoholism, we feel it necessary to clarify that although our approach to this problem differs from the model most often used, we nevertheless recognize that excessive drinking can and does have an enormous effect on the health and survival of the drinker and often catastrophic effects on others. Our effort in this book is not to downplay the seriousness of this impact but to offer an alternative approach that can change this kind of problem more effectively and efficiently. We do not claim to have a surefire method of dealing with undesired drinking, but the case described in this chapter is an example of how brief interventions can bring about enduring changes in drinking practices.

SOME NOTIONS ABOUT DRINKING

Attitudes about excessive drinking always have had moralistic associations. We suppose this has had to do with the fact that unlike most other social problems, excessive drinking requires the drinker to knowingly make himself a spectacle of irresponsible and unpredictable behavior, that is, to drink to inebriation. (Of course, some allowances are made for New Year's Eve celebrations and some forms of male group drinking, e.g., bachelor parties, although some people define excessive drinking even in these settings as forms of alcoholism.)

In earlier centuries, excessive drinking was looked on as a weakness of character or as evidence of the basic evils of the drinker, who had succumbed to temptations by the devil, the "Demon Rum." In more recent times, excessive drinking has become defined as an illness, thereby helping to relieve the excessive drinker from the traditional moral opprobrium of the drunkard. The illness label implies that the afflicted person is a victim of an unwanted condition. One of the inherent difficulties created by these labels is that they imply relative unchangeability: they focus on what a person *is* instead of what a person *does*.

SOME OBSTACLES TO CHANGE

A central theme running through the work of the Brief Therapy Center is *change*. Therefore, we are sensitive to assumptions about people and their problems that imply unchangeability, fixedness, "they way things are." These assumptions can be as simple as "He is a . . . " in contrast to "He does . . . " It is harder to consider changing the way a person is than it is to change what that person does. For a number of human problems, the unchangeability is usually attributed to some biological factor, such as genetic predisposition or some unexplained anomaly of metabolism. The medicalizing of human problems has become more and more the fashion. Thus it has become standard to inquire about such things as suicide, depression, markedly changing moods, and, of course, excessive drinking, in a client's family of origin or extended family. The implicit assumption in such inquiry is that if any of those factors were present in the nuclear or extended family, then the client is predisposed to similar problems. Social, economic, and cultural factors are given less weight in favor of some genetic explanation.

This approach equally tends to obscure the role of personal decisions and behavior. Even as it absolves people from their influence on themselves and each other, it defines the client as a victim, with all the implications this can have: helplessness and limitations on the client's ability to change his predicament. This viewpoint seems to have become established as an unquestionable truth so that investigating excessive drinking from a very different viewpoint is considered a kind of heresy. Therapists challenging the prevailing view run the risk of being accused of trivializing the pain and suffering of family members of an excessive drinker.

The problem with the current view is that "treatment" is lifelong and sets apart from mainstream society the person who has drunk excessively. She does not simply *have* a problem, she *is* a problem in the sense that her problem is a strong component in defining who she is. The cost of alleviation is for her to accept her identity as revolving around her stigma. It is this strict adherence to abstinence and the commitment to it by the client that has discouraged many excessive drinkers from seeking help. Some, too, are alienated by Alcoholic Anonymous's emphasis on accepting a higher power as a necessity in its program (see Shute, 1997).

WHO IS THE COMPLAINANT?

As with all other kinds of problems, we look at undesired drinking as a *behavior* that someone is complaining about. As in a number of problems, the one who is complained about, the drinker, is less often the complainant than is a family member or boss or an agent of social control (probation officer, Child Protective Services personnel, the police, and the like). When an individual arranges to see a therapist, he is often not a complainant about his own behavior but has been coerced to seek therapy; he is an involuntary client. We can determine this rather early in an initial session by asking the client what precipitated his decision to call or walk in for help. A characteristic response is, "Well, I really tied on one last weekend, and Sunday evening my wife told me she will see a lawyer for divorce unless I get some help with my drinking. So I called you Monday." In such a case, we would want to see the client's wife, as it is fairly obvious that she is the complainant about his drinking, not he, and we would need to know how she has tried to get him to alter his drinking.

Although attempted solutions can take various forms—hunting for bottles and throwing them away, exhorting her husband to attend AA, making critical remarks when he takes another drink, asking his friends to "reason" with him, and so on—with few exceptions, they convey to the drinker, "You must, and can, stop drinking!" We have hypothesized that this approach frequently doesn't work because it consists of a Don't command as opposed to a Do command. The case we present illustrates this formulation.

"I WANT TO BE A CONTROLLED DRINKER"

Considering the prevailing model for treating excessive drinking, we were interested when Judy asked for help with her drinking and said that she was hoping she could come to drink "normally" (that is, to engage in controlled, social, nonproblem drinking). She was thirty-one, married, with two young children. She had worked outside the home in a professional capacity, but in recent years had restricted her work to taking care of the family and managing their home. Her husband, George, worked as a business consultant. Judy had been seeing a therapist who had agreed to help with her desire to become a "normal" drinker, but after a year there was no change, and her therapist gave her our name.

Her first therapist had attempted to have her use the idea that she always had a choice regarding her drinking; i.e., she could *choose* to drink or not drink just as she could choose to stop at any number of drinks. With this theme in mind, the therapist asked Judy to schedule how many drinks she might have as well as schedule periods of abstinence. For some brief periods, Judy would white-knuckle abstinence, but when the "sentence" was finished, she would revert to excessive drinking rather than stick to scheduling her drinking. Thus, although her therapist was willing to pursue a novel goal, she was still using one of the most common attempted solutions: "You must not drink!"

As you will see, Judy gave a fairly succinct statement of the problem: drinking. As with any problem, we do not think in normative terms, that is, whether a behavior deviates from some standard of normality; rather, we are interested in what the client regards as a problem for herself. Thus, we ask about such things as the quantity of alcohol she drinks not to determine whether or not Judy is an alcoholic but to find out what *she* regards as problem drinking. Her comments about drinking affecting her liver and interfering with sex and about her becoming more irritable with the children are more to the point. Of course, much of this information could have been elicited with the simple question, "How is your drinking a problem for *you*?"

Session One

The therapist saw Judy alone in the first session. In this segment, Judy indicated her interest in altering her drinking by learning to control it rather than by becoming a teetotaler.

> THERAPIST: What's the problem?
> JUDY: Drinking.
> THERAPIST: Can you fill me in a little more about that? What's the problem with it?
> JUDY: The problem is, I guess, that I . . . oh, I guess always tended to be . . . not really a heavy, heavy drinker, but I always was the one who wanted to go out and have a good time, I guess, and have always enjoyed having drinks and going out. But it began to be a problem about two years ago when I started drinking by myself or felt like I had to have drinks every night, and

about a year ago it got to the point where I knew I needed something. The doctor said that he could tell that my drinking was affecting my liver.

THERAPIST: Did he say how?

JUDY: He just said I had some fat in my liver. He took blood tests and said, very clinically, "You are not a person who can tolerate alcohol. You should never drink again. If you have trouble with that, see a counselor." See ya later! I was hurt and resentful and did not quit drinking.

THERAPIST: When you say, "I'm drinking too much," what would be characteristic of that?

JUDY: Well, drinking every night. Drinking like a bottle of wine or more every night. It does not matter the quantity, really; it's a matter that it is affecting my life, the relationship with my husband. I'm wasting evenings. I'm not being productive. Other priorities that I had are . . . reading has gone away now.

THERAPIST: You said that at your level of drinking, it's affecting your life and also your health. Can you fill me in as to how it's affecting you in those ways?

JUDY: When I have a night of heavy drinking, I am in pain in the liver area the next morning. I was supposed to be rechecked but never went back. I have not had regular periods in two years. I also know it bothers my husband a lot. It's not real great for our sex life. I think I feel bad about myself, so I am harsher on the children.

THERAPIST: Why now?

JUDY: I was visiting my parents recently, and one night when I was there I had too much to drink, and we went on a walk after dinner, and I was not walking straight, out of balance; my speech was a little slurred. It has happened before when I was there, but they really confronted me with that. I told them what I was doing to stop, and they said it would not work. "You have to understand that you can never drink again." It was really parent to child. "This is what you have to do!"

THERAPIST: Since we work in a relatively short period of time, it would save an awful lot of time if we could know what you have done or George has done in an attempt to resolve this problem for you that has not worked or has not worked well enough. That is, if we can know from the start what not to bother with, it can save a heck of a lot of time. So let me check with you now as to what you or anybody else concerned about the problem has been trying to do, advise?

JUDY: Yes, right. Briefly, you always have a choice. My therapist would try to get me to make choices. She would say, "Go out and choose not to drink. Or, if you had one drink, choose whether to have another one or not." I, basically, was choosing, and I was choosing to have a drink! My therapist also said that I was drinking to help me relax, so she said that at the health food store you can get herbal tea, which didn't do much. (*Laughs*) She would also tell George to make it my problem and not to make it his. He should just leave the room or walk away while I was doing this and it bothered him. George has taken every approach he can. He is very understanding. He has gotten angry with me.

THERAPIST: [Was there] anything else [the therapist said] that he should do or suggested that he should do as part of making it your problem?

JUDY: She just said to try and ignore what I was doing. Since then, he has gone different ways. He has done everything from not mentioning anything to really confronting me with it.

"Done everything from not mentioning anything to really confronting me" represents a common misunderstanding by clients that *not saying something* is a change, a significant change. From our viewpoint, this behavior isn't a change at all. When another person has taken a definite position, in this case, "You've drunk too much!" their *not* saying it is likely to leave the impression that the person's position hasn't changed but is only on hold: "He's not saying it, but he is still thinking it. He's likely to scold me for drinking later today or tomorrow."

THERAPIST: What does he say when he confronts you?

JUDY: Well, it's usually in the morning. He will say either something sarcastic like, "You were a real gem last night," or "What did you have to drink!? How did you get so in the bag?" Something like that. "Is there something I can do?"

THERAPIST: Anything else that you have tried in an attempt to eliminate or reduce your drinking?

JUDY: I really thought that I would try to feel good about myself, to feel like I am in control. What I wanted to do was to set a month of not drinking, then go for another month, another two weeks or whatever. My goals would be short term rather than long term. I went for about one and a half weeks I guess. And then we went out for something or other, and I had some drinks, and then I tried to resolve again, and I went for a couple of days and then let go. "You've got to end this, you've got to end it!" And it is making me more panicked and, consequently, I've been drinking almost more, thinking that this is going to be it, this is going to be the last. "Tomorrow I will not drink anything more, so I can have whatever I want tonight." You know what I mean? This has been the biggest problem that I have had.

In this segment, the therapist elicited features of Judy's attempted solution. We used to ask, "What doesn't work?" but realized that this question could imply that other things the client had tried *did* work.

We include temporary or partial effectiveness in the "not working" category, because we believe that if a client is seeking professional help it means that whatever seemingly positive changes have occurred, the change is insufficient: the client still has a complaint. Clients also believe that whatever they have done that makes for a temporary or partial improvement is a useful and dependable direction, a notion that can interfere with their option of taking a very different direction. Thus, we now are accustomed to asking, "What doesn't work or doesn't work well enough?"

We have found that methods requiring individuals to wrestle with the temptation to partake of whatever it is they are concerned about (alcoholic drinks, candy and other "forbidden" sweets, street drugs) usually results in their giving in to the temptation. We have speculated that the apparently simple act of struggling with temptation is likely to lose because it sets up a Don't command if one is to resist the temptation while it simultaneously offers a Do command presented by the unwanted substance itself; i.e., we find it a reliable notion that one cannot comply with a Don't command unless there is an alternative Do command.

Thus, Nancy Reagan's "Just say no to drugs" is unlikely to work unless there is also an "Instead say yes to [something other than the drug]." In the struggle between "I'm tempted" and "but I must *not* give in," the temptation is, logically, a much easier command to follow. One cannot stop sitting unless permitted to do something different, be it standing, lying down, slumping to the floor, or whatever, as an *alternative* action.

Our colleague John Frykman, who some years ago worked with heroin addicts in the Haight Ashbury section of San Francisco, instituted this principle in treating his clients, with surprisingly effective and durable results. In effect, he gave them a simple alternative action to take when they were confronted by the temptation to shoot up. First, he summarized, graphically, all those factors that previously led to the client's reusing heroin—losing his job, peer pressure, learning of a close friend's death or near death from overuse of a drug, seeking comfort from a girlfriend or other close person who, instead, offered him a free shot of heroin. Next, Frykman asked the client, "If, at that high point of temptation, you had said, 'No, thank you' to the friend, turned on your heels, and walked out, would that tell you anything about resistance to further use?" Although this question was presented as a way for the "addict" to determine whether he had overcome his "habit," it has built into it an implicit suggestion for an alternative action: say "no, thank you" and then turn on your heels and walk out; if you do that, you will be in control of temptation. We attribute the effectiveness of Frykman's approach to its offering the "junkie" an immediate and simple alternative to giving in to temptation.

Judy mentions another suggestion, drinking herbal tea as a substitute for alcohol. Drinking tea would seem to suffice as an alternative action, but it is the kind of alternative that tends to maintain the client's struggle with temptation because, as a substitute, it can reinforce the desirability of the "real thing." At the same time, it is not a readily available alternative. It might be more effective if a cup or pot of herbal tea were within easy and immediate reach. A better alternative would be some action; for example, "When you are tempted, go out the door and take a brisk walk to *strengthen* your body rather than *weaken* it." In addition to avoiding the framing of a substitute, this alternative puts the emphasis on doing something for one's body, not simply escaping from an urge.

In principle, the therapist's advice to Judy's husband—to make Judy's drinking her problem and presumably not his—could be useful and effective. However, suggesting he do this by leaving the house nullified its effectiveness because his leaving runs too high a risk of being seen as an expression of condemnation of Judy's drinking and, in that way, maintains the understanding that her drinking bothered him. Also, suggesting he ignore her drinking is another form of a Don't command. So are "*not* confronting" and "*not* mentioning anything" Empirically, we and other therapists have found that trying to ignore a disagreeable event rarely works. In any case, these suggestions did not interdict his well-meant "confrontations," which consisted of angry or rhetorical critical comments.

Judy's own efforts to control her drinking, mainly by setting periods of time when she resolved not to drink, didn't work either, we believe for the reasons we have already discussed. Again, these are different forms of trying to use a No or Don't command, which keep the struggle alive until the person exhaustedly gives in to the Do of drinking. We were not surprised that these white-knuckle efforts resulted in Judy's drinking more. In traditional approaches to the problem, these suggestions are considered eminently reasonable, and the failure of the drinker to succeed with them is explained as evidence of addiction. In our view, even though these methods are "commonsensical" and echo common logic, they are nevertheless unwitting ways of *maintaining* the problem.

As we see in the next dialogue, Judy also expressed her dilemma about how to resolve her problem. On the one hand, she felt she couldn't argue with the advice of others that it would require abstinence; on the other hand, "emotionally" she still felt strongly that she could bring her drinking under control. Because we do not use traditional concepts of excessive drinking as a disease, we are free to consider that what she wants is possible.

> JUDY: *(Resuming previous dialogue)* . . . This has been the biggest problem I have had.
> THERAPIST: Not sticking to the goals you have set?
> JUDY: Right. This has been a real problem. I think, intellectually, I know that to solve the problem by myself is going to have to be quitting drinking altogether but, emotionally, I never want to give in to that because I am a strong person, and I always thought, "I have been able to control other things in my life; I can control this." I have never wanted to admit to myself that I had to stop altogether.

Here is a clear example of what we call the client's *position*. In our view, getting people to depart from the way they are trying to deal with their problem is the main task of therapy—not an easy task, because they and most others consider what they are doing to be the only reasonable thing to do. In a manner of speaking, we are often attempting to get people to depart from logic, reasonableness, sanity, if you will.

We have found it helpful to frame the "illogical" alternative in a way that incorporates the way the client sees herself and the problem. Judy stated plainly and firmly that she saw herself as a strong person, in control of herself and the events of her life. The therapist used Judy's self-perception as an opportunity to offer her an additional option for dealing with her desired level of drinking.

> THERAPIST: Some people who have had trouble control-ling their drinking have been able to control it to the point where they have become social drinkers, but it takes a really *strong person* to do that. It is by *no means the majority of people who can do that*. I am just saying that you feel you really need to stop altogether because it has been very hard to admit that—
> JUDY: Right. That has to be the answer.
> THERAPIST: —that you are not one of those *exceptional peo-ple* who can bring about *full control*.

The words shown here in italics echoed and spoke to Judy's own position. They framed the attainment of her wish as a challenge; in any case, urging abstinence had not worked.

> JUDY: Yes, I guess what I'm looking for are the tools to put myself in control; to feel like I don't have to drink to be social, to be with people. To feel in control, I don't need the drinking.

Session Two

Rather than wait, we felt it important to engage George in the ther-apy before seeing Judy again, and, as is our custom, we saw him alone for the second session. His definition of the problem echoed Judy's, and we proceeded to ask how he has tried to get her to stop drinking.

> THERAPIST: I would appreciate it if you gave me your own picture as to what is the problem. How would you describe it?

GEORGE: Well, the problem, to put it briefly, is almost precisely as you stated it previously; that Judy has a tendency to, number one, drink alone now; two, when she [drinks] with others, drinks to excess, almost always and I think once she realized that she had a problem, that put additional pressure on her with respect to alcohol, and rather than cutting down or quitting, she's gone just the other way. I think probably the major effect is that it angers me, and I have tried to control that and be understanding, but there is just no question. It just plain upsets me, and it manifests itself in anger.

THERAPIST: When you do get angry, how do you convey it? What do you do, what do you say? That kind of thing.

GEORGE: What I usually did was to make a couple of snide remarks; not something I would normally do. I do not do that as much anymore. I found that it does no good at all for me to jump down Judy's throat, particularly if she's been drinking. It just gets me more frustrated. What I do now, typically, is go somewhere else, in the other room, sit down and read, listen to music or something like that. It starts to affect the way I trust Judy. On this one area, I can't trust her anymore. I know she's going to be off sneaking drinks, so I feel like I always have to watch her. I am very concerned that she is going to be drinking and driving either by herself or, even worse, taking a drive with our children. I feel like the trust in our relationship has gone down quite a bit.

THERAPIST: You mentioned that at the time when you are home you'd go off to a cupboard where there's a hidden bottle; is that one of the things you've tried? To look for hidden bottles? Do you throw them out, or what?

GEORGE: Yeah. Oh, yes.

Here, George clearly described how he had tried to influence Judy to stop drinking. You can probably see how pervasive this influence can be. With the kind and frequency of his comments, his very presence could serve as a critical reminder of her drinking. Even though he realized his efforts had been fruitless, if not counterproductive, George persevered with them because he was at a loss as to what else he could do. In essence, he repeatedly conveyed to her, "You must stop drinking!" by taking a position of engaging in surveillance and monitoring her behavior. (We might say that his efforts produced the contradictory "You must forget what I will continuously remind you of." This, of course, is conjecture, and we would not assume that the problem was maintained by this contradiction. We prefer to proceed on the basis that *whatever* the persistent attempt at solution, *that* is the unwitting fuel that maintains the problem. In that sense, the "why" of it is not relevant.)

Before the next session, we felt we had enough information to focus on George's attempted solution and we believed it played a significant part in Judy's preoccupation with drinking. Knowing that he was highly skeptical of Judy's ability to become a controlled drinker and that Judy was hanging on to that goal, we considered using George's skepticism to tempt her to drink, thus departing from his attempted solution.

Session Three

We met with both Judy and George in the third session. We suggested a task as a test of Judy's ability to control her drinking. The stated purpose of the "test" was to determine whether she could really do it or, failing the test, commit herself to the necessity of resolving the problem through abstention, rather than waver between the two approaches. As we hoped, this framing satisfied George. As a next step . . .

> THERAPIST: *(To George)* However it is you may want to go about it, in dealing with her problem one of your best roles in it would be to not make it easy for her. Otherwise, whatever she might accomplish wouldn't be reliable.

Because George and Judy accepted this role, we laid out the specifics of the test. Judy was to set her own limit, on a daily basis, of what controlling her drinking would mean. However, in not making it easy for her, George was to encourage her to drink more than her limit; we said that he could do it explicitly ("You look like you could relax; how about a drink?") or implicitly.

Our allowing George to make it hard for Judy in an implicit way was intended to blunt her interpreting a look of impatience or disapproval as discouraging her from drinking by interposing a doubt as to whether George's look was part of the strategy to *encourage* her to drink. We thought it would be important to give her some way of avoiding being implicitly provoked to drink beyond her own set goal.

We decided to use what we saw in hindsight to be a form of ordeal used by Milton Erickson and Jay Haley in their clinical work. That is, if on any day she did go over her limit, she and George were to plan on some enforced drinking over the weekend. We were hopeful about the idea because George would be the enforcer (he was to pour a bottle of wine out into separate glasses and insist she drink them up, one at a time) and therefore quite clearly departing from "You must stop drinking." As it turned out, we didn't have a chance to see how this idea would have worked.

> JUDY: It seems like a game, and neither George nor I are game players. If he decides he can go along with it, I think I could go along with it, although, I guess . . . you know . . . I agree it seems rather bizarre. Several things, though . . .
>
> THERAPIST: Of course the game of sneaking drinks is not bizarre. (*Judy laughs.*)
>
> THERAPIST: You're right, it is a game, and (*To George*) you've been playing the game of trying to check. But this is a different game.

Later in that session:

GEORGE: Yes. I'm definitely willing to go along with anything that might make a change, with anything that's worth trying. I sure am definitely willing to go along with it. I can't see that anything else has worked.

Session Four

In session four, we learned from the couple that the program didn't get under way because they had gotten their signals mixed up, and they abandoned it. We framed their confusion as their having tried to proceed without first looking ahead at the possible disadvantages of resolving the problem; rather than fault them for abandoning the program, we defined their error as a legitimate alert to those possible disadvantages. Thus, we asked them to think over and discuss between them what could be the full impact of eliminating the problem, especially if it were resolved through controlled drinking on Judy's part.

Raising the question of the possible disadvantages of improvement has several uses. First of all, clients are often prone to assuming that resolution of their problems will be an unmixed blessing, and this question allows them to anticipate the possibility of unpleasant events that can result from a change, even a desired change. We do not believe that a problem serves a needed function for the individual or the family but, rather, that when one thing changes, it can stimulate other changes in people's lives. (For example, when a teenager's behavior becomes more acceptable to others, the teenager may enhance his commitment to other people outside the family and thus decrease his involvement within the family, something that Mom and Dad hadn't considered.)

Session Five

The therapist again met with both Judy and George in the fifth session.

THERAPIST: . . . so I'm interested in what your thoughts are.
GEORGE: OK, I wrote them down. The first thing we thought of, and there's no priority to this is . . . I think we're

both concerned that if Judy were to stop drinking it could, in some way, curtail both our social lives, because our social lives tend to revolve, in one way or another, with drinking. . . . We're afraid we might be less likely to socialize . . . or that the socializing might be less fun or whatever. . . .

This is one we listed as a possible. You asked us to list whatever we could think of, and we wonder if maybe we're not both happy with the role of me watching Judy and Judy being the person who's being watched. If Judy were to stop drinking or to control her drinking and solve the problem, we would no longer have the roles we've exercised over the last couple of years. . . . The disadvantage would be we that we're both comfortable in those roles; now we may have to assume no roles or different roles.

Another one is, when we drink together, when the two of us drink, we communicate much better for whatever reasons; after four martinis, after a glass of wine or two, we both tend to come out of whatever shells we've been in from everyday life, and we're afraid that if one person stops there may be a communication gap, that neither of us will come out of our shell and we'll sit there in the evening and not say a word to each other.

Now this is another one that we thought of; I may be, I think I am afraid that if Judy were to quit drinking or would control her drinking, I would have to be her caretaker in a different way. It's much easier for me to have Judy drinking and not have to worry about her drinking than it is for me to constantly have to watch her, be constantly on the watch.

THERAPIST: I'm not clear about that, George.

GEORGE: If she were to stop, the disadvantage to me is whenever she's done that in the past it's made me wonder, "Is she drinking now or isn't she? Is she sneaking drinks at the party?" She says she's going to control it, and I immediately start watching her all the time, which drives her crazy. It drives me crazy. The thing is that in the past when she has stopped drinking, she's much more likely to be in a bad mood; she's generally in a good mood, but I don't think there's any question that if she stopped drinking, in the initial periods she would not be particularly in a good mood. Now whether that would last twenty-four hours or twenty-four days or twenty-four months, I don't know. But that's been our experience.

THERAPIST: *(Responding to a phone call from the observation room)* Yes, John Weakland was saying there's a converse problem that, uh, there could be a problem. . . . If you felt that she *isn't* abusing [alcohol]. You might, therefore, have to take more legitimately her point in a discussion than you had before, and this could be a problem for you.

Later in that session, the therapist added the team's speculation that especially if she resolved the problem through controlling her drinking, "doing it the hard way," it would upset the balance of the one-up and one-down relationship they had seemed to work out over the years—that her current drinking served as a well-meant "rescue operation" of that balance. (It would seem from this comment that we adhere to the notion that a problem serves a needed function. However, this thought was offered only to confirm the validity of asking what problems might arise from a change in Judy's drinking.)

JUDY: As a matter of fact, it's always been interesting to me that you've wanted to see us together, since it's my problem, not George's. Why should he stop work and come up here? I think you've put into words for me the things I've been trying to gel since we started this whole thing. I went to a coffee last week, and they were talking about a weight-loss program, "Thin Within." One of their premises is that you get yourself in the position like "Now I'm overweight," and it sort of dominates your life. The whole drinking and weight thing is on my mind constantly.

This session ended with the recommendation that they both think over the impact of changing the problem and whether or not to pursue its resolution.

Sessions Six Through Nine

We were assuming George and Judy would want to go ahead with the previously worked out test, but in the following session, Judy presented us with a surprise. She was pregnant! The cessation of her periods was not from any metabolic disturbance, at least not a pathological one, but from a more natural cause. After we consulted with her obstetrician, we decided to abandon the test, as any addition to her alcohol intake could further jeopardize the health of the fetus.

We still felt that George's role in the problem played a strategic part, and we met with him on the following appointment (session seven). It's not by default that we decided to focus on George's participation in the problem rather than on Judy's. We felt that George was the more active player in making an effort to change Judy's drinking behavior and that therefore he had the best leverage in intervening in their vicious cycle.

Because we saw George alone in the seventh, eighth, and ninth sessions, we took up with him, directly, the counterproductive role of his playing watchdog. We summarized the different ways he did that and how it relieved Judy of the responsibility for her drinking by implying that the problem belonged to him. He agreed and said he would make an effort to depart from the role. However, we weren't sure how clearly he understood the importance of departing from monitoring her drinking, nor how consistently he would implement it.

GEORGE: She's still controlling it much better than when we came here. She's not controlling it quite as well since two weeks ago; that is, she was controlling it much better when she picked a goal each day and stuck to it. Which is not to say she's really ever hit the point, almost daily. One night this week, she was visibly under the influence of alcohol. Other than that she's been pretty successful through January but not as good as she was up to two weeks ago . . . until then, her drinking was very controlled. At no time was she under the influence until that one time we went to the Christmas party.

THERAPIST: During the month of December, you say she was cooling it quite recognizably. I was wondering if during that time you were departing from your old way of trying to deal with it.

GEORGE: Oh, yeah! Absolutely.

THERAPIST: He [a team observer] said that you commented that in these last two weeks, while Judy is controlling it rather well, it is not quite as good as in the previous two weeks and that this was making you nervous. He was wondering if in your ner-vousness had you gone a bit back to the older tack.

GEORGE: Yes.

THERAPIST: All right . . .

GEORGE: . . . Yeah, it's something I try to avoid, but it's difficult for me to avoid it. The downsides are nowhere near as bad as they . . . much less frequently . . . than they used to be and the ups are for a longer period . . . so there's a definite improvement.

The therapist and the treatment team felt that the most strate-gic element in the therapy was the change in George's handling of Judy's drinking, mainly his departure from his customary watchdog position. In retrospect, we saw that we had underestimated him. We had planned to see him in that ninth session because we felt he had not gotten the idea of how his dealing with Judy's drinking played a strategic role in her drinking practice. Yet near the start of that session, he informed us that he had quite clearly "gotten it" and that during that prior month she was controlling her drinking. This would have meant her improvement predated the discovery of her pregnancy. Almost as an accidental experiment, when he panicked following her intoxication at the Christmas party and reverted to his former watchdog position, her control of her drinking deteriorated, at least temporarily, notwithstanding that she was aware of her pregnant state by that time.

We felt that he had a clear enough understanding of the process. We hoped that with an understanding of his role and of how he could slip back, George would be able to maintain a more consistent response. There was one session left of our ten-session limit, and we and George agreed that rather than use it at that time, it would be left in the bank should he or Judy feel the need for another session.

Follow-Up

As is customary in all our cases, we conducted a three-month follow-up evaluation. As for their concern about her drinking, Judy said it had decreased, George adding, "The problem seems to have diminished to quite a degree." George had backed off from his watchdog position and he used the qualifier "to a large extent." As an example of backing off, he said that before he would count how many drinks she had and would watch the liquor cabinet. Now, he rarely did it. There were no new problems and there had been no further therapy for either of them.

We also conducted a one-year follow-up. At that time, Judy's concern about her drinking had further diminished, which she attributed to having had a new child.

George's report was still somewhat equivocal. On the one hand, he expressed concern that, on occasion, she was still sneaking drinks and getting drunk, but he qualified that by saying such incidences were not as acute nor as frequent as they used to be. Overall, he felt she was doing better. When asked about his backing off from surveillance of her drinking, he said that he had backed off "some, but not totally, not as much as I should, I suppose." He guessed about 60 percent. There were no new problems, and neither of them had sought any further therapy.

Because of what seemed to be his tenuous adherence to avoiding watchdogging, we asked George if he would like to make use of the last session, which was being held in the bank for them. He said he didn't feel it necessary. It is possible it might have been better if we had simply asked him to come in so that he and we would have a chance to see what induced the "slipping" and to determine how that might be better handled.

We tend to avoid asking people to come in, especially if they are not initiating it or are, as in this case, resisting it. We want to avoid implicitly framing any further therapy as being for our benefit, not the client's—that we have "owned" the problem. George said he felt it wasn't necessary but would avail himself of it if things became shaky.

Because the Brief Therapy Center is, primarily, a clinical research project rather than a service project, there were a number of features in our experience with Judy and George that interested us. Primary among them was the strategic influence exerted by diverting George from his customary way of handling her drinking, his attempted solution. Although Judy was also a complainant about her own drinking, George had more significant impact on the problem. Second, we would have been more assured of continuing success for them if the change had not been described as a quantitative one ("less frequent," "better than before"). Related to that, the change in George's attempted solution was also quantitative ("I'm doing less of it," "60 percent").

A clear departure from a client's attempted solution usually is accompanied by a new behavior. We operate on the principle that a person can't stop performing a behavior without performing an alternative and, preferably, a qualitatively different behavior. If our research design were not restricted to a ten-session limit, we likely would have extended the therapy for the purpose of giving "booster shots" to George and attempted to have him take a more unequivocal departure from his traditional attempts, likely in the direction of *encouraging* Judy to drink.

As we said at the beginning of the chapter, we presented this case not as a formula for brief resolution of drinking problems but rather as an indicator that substantial change *can* occur in a relatively short time, and without the necessity for abstention. We see this work as the beginning of further research in this knotty class of problems (see Shute, 1997). We also feel that further research is needed to integrate the experiences and perspectives of therapists with other social scientists; anthropologists and sociologists come to mind. For example, how does the drinking of an alcoholic beverage as an introduction to a social encounter become a practice (e.g., the early offering of a drink to guests at one's home, or the establishment of the café and bar as centers of socializing); how does this differ from culture to culture, and are differences reflected in the incidence of excessive drinking?

The cases we have looked at so far in this book have in common that many therapists regard the problems as serious or intimidating because the problems have potentially catastrophic outcomes and because they have been resistant to psychotherapeutic change. Working briefly with such cases is often regarded as naive, at best.

The cases in the next three chapters are different in that the problems usually pose little or no potential risk of dramatic catastrophe. However, we include them in this book because the features of those problems have such grave effects on the clients' lives. Their "symptoms" come to rule the individuals' everyday lives economically and socially, and in forming and maintaining relationships. These factors tend to make these problems intimidating to the therapist. In the first such case, the client's life had become a directionless and meaningless morass; psychologically, he was inundated with almost continuous compulsions to perform a variety of crippling rituals; physically, his milieu was a home inundated with mountains of meaningless paper. In the second case, the client had struggled with problems of drug abuse, subsequent imprisonment, and the sudden collapse of her marriage; in the ensuing carnage of events she had become a recluse, barely leaving her home, spending four days each week sleeping, and surviving on a subsistence economic support. In traditional nosology she would have been diagnosed as depressed, phobic, and probably schizoid, with an underlying character disorder. In a final case, a young woman had compulsively disfigured herself, which had seriously threatened her career as well as her personal relationships and health.

Although each of these cases are qualitatively different from the preceding ones, they are, nevertheless, examples of problems that can be catastrophic in the slow degradation of the individuals' ability to survive. These kinds of problems often are also intimidating to the psychotherapist. We therefore felt that these cases would be appropriate examples of the possibility of durable change by means of brief problem-solving therapy.

6

Incapacitating Problems
Obsessive-Compulsive Behavior

We present this type of problem not because it has the catastrophic effects of other problems we have treated but
because of the incapacitating effects it can have in the client's life
and because many therapists don't trust their expertise to deal with
it. Many therapists often end up referring "OCD" cases to psychiatrists so that these clients might be given medications.

In our view, problems, for the most part, are behaviors undesired
by the client, and accordingly we consider it more to the point to
deal with those behaviors than with a label. Diagnostic labels also
tend to discourage therapists and lend an implicit pessimism in therapy. OCD (Obsessive-Compulsive Disorder) is one of those currently fashionable acronyms.

KIRK

Kirk was a thirty-five-year-old unmarried biologist who sought help
because he was having considerable difficulty getting on with his
writing.

Session One

The therapist began the session with our usual question.

> THERAPIST: What is the problem? What is the trouble that
> brings you in today?

KIRK: I have quit my teaching job and am purposely unemployed so that I can write up some scientific ideas that I have for scientific journals, which requires library research on my own. These articles would also be for the general public. I want to be my own boss and write, but I get distracted by other things. I'll read the *Nature Club Bulletin* or the newspaper; I jog, and it goes into an hour and fifteen minutes; maybe talk on the phone with someone; maybe read junk mail that is not completely junk mail—it's interesting junk mail, like magazines or something that I can tell myself in a way I am doing the work when I am actually obviously goofing off or reading junk mail. I seem to need to do things that are barely related to my goal, at best, or not even related at all. I just kind of fool myself.

THERAPIST: The goal being doing research?

KIRK: And the writing, right. Writing up the research. I use up my time, and the whole day is gone, and then I vow not to do the same thing again, and then it happens again the next day. I have a real tendency to get caught up in detail. I am an obsessive-compulsive. When I read, I say the word "fine," and then I read the first word in the sentence. For example, if it's "the," I'll go, "fine, the, fine, the." I will do that several times before I read the sentence. Or other things like that when I read. That is just one example.

Or things that I feel that I have to do to feel comfortable, and if I don't do that I feel some discomfort.

THERAPIST: The word "fine" being there?

KIRK: Just a word that I make up. Or if I close a door, I push on it three times to make sure it's closed, even though I know it's closed. I feel uncomfortable if I do not get into the details of these peripherals. If it is mailed to me, I feel like I have to read it, even though I know it is a waste of my time.

Here is a good example of the advantages of not proceeding with a label—OCD—but instead focusing on "What's the problem?" If we had asked him sooner, as we usually do, "*How* is it a problem for you?" he would have then talked about his earnest wish to get on with his research and writing and his failure to do that. His discourse on his obsessive and compulsive behavior, in that case, would have been an *explanation* for the problem, not a problem in itself. If writing or some other venture was not important to him, it is likely that his rituals would not have been a problem for him.

Over time, we have realized that many people interpret the question "What's the problem?" to mean that we are asking for the underlying reason or explanation for the trouble they are struggling with. Now we more often ask "What's the problem, that is, what's the trouble you are having that brings you in?" because this clarifies what we are asking about. Asking clients *how* an unfortunate-sounding state of affairs is a problem for them can often reveal or clarify exactly what it is they are having trouble with. Sometimes it will open up a new option for resolving a problem that would have been obscured by focusing on the state of affairs itself.

Our colleague John Weakland interviewed a woman who stated her problem as having recently discovered that her husband was having an almost daily affair with a neighbor woman rather than going off to work as she had assumed. When Weakland asked her how this was a problem for her, she said that the family finances were in dreadful condition, and because her husband's income was directly proportional to the amount of time he spent at work, "He's wasting income-earning time on that floozy around the corner!" On further questioning, she confirmed that that was the problem she was concerned about, not his philandering per se. "If it weren't for the money, it's OK if he wants to waste his time with her. I've got better things to do." This clarification expanded options for resolution beyond getting her husband to stop the affair. For example, she could strike a "deal" with him to balance time spent with the other woman and with work—"How about Wednesdays and weekends with her?"

This kind of focalizing also reflects the difference between a model that is complaint-based and one that is normative. Diagnosis is consistent with models that reflect a concept of normal and abnormal, and those models, thereby, have the potential for expanding the parameters of the therapy and, thus, lengthening it. A complaint-based model does not incorporate such a viewpoint but instead bases the therapy around behaviors undesired by the particular individual, without judging whether that complaint is legitimate or not. Therefore, whatever might be otherwise considered abnormal is regarded as irrelevant; this is a significant factor in making therapy briefer.

THERAPIST: In defining yourself as an obsessive-compulsive, how is that related to your not being able to focus on the reading that you need to do and the writing, now?

KIRK: First, it takes me much longer to read something than it should because I have these rituals when I read, like the one I described, or I reread a paragraph to make sure I have it. It slows down my work. I would like to deal with that with this program; but, also, it isn't that I get caught up in details, it is a part of my OC. I feel a compulsive need to read things that I don't really need to read. If they are somewhat interesting, if it is sent to me and it has my name on it, I feel obligated to read it. Or if there is something in the newspaper that is relevant, somewhat, then I have to give it my time. And when I jog, I cannot just jog forty-five minutes; I have to jog one hour and fifteen minutes.

THERAPIST: You say this has been going on for a while. What have you tried, in your best efforts, to change the situation? We are particularly interested in the ones that have not worked.

KIRK: I have been to many different therapies and have gotten a lot out of it in other ways, but it hasn't worked with this.

THERAPIST: Trying to sit down to read and do the writing?

KIRK: Yes. It has not worked well at all. I have done various things that I hoped would help. I tried transcendental meditation and whatever. I've tried hypnosis, not really with this in mind;

read books like *Control Your Time and Life*, by Laken; things like making schedules and daily to-do lists, and that worked to a limited extent. I think that what did not work is that I did not really carry it out. Deadlines and schedules, I did not give that a fair shot in spite of the fact that it started to work some.

When a client says that something started to work or worked partially but that he didn't continue with it, you may be tempted to assume that this reflects a lack of effort. A further assumption, often, is that the client doesn't really want to get over the stated problem—that there is some kind of hidden agenda or that the problem serves some needed function for the individual or the family.

We prefer to assume that the plan, logical as it might seem, simply does not work for that particular client and instead may be part of his attempted solution. We do not rule out the need to be alert to a client who is entering into therapy on a pro forma basis. But in those cases, there is often corroborating information. For example, the client will have indicated that the therapy was not his idea but someone else's, such as that of a spouse or an agent of social control. The client will also give minimal responses to questions seeking information, answering many with "I don't know" or "I forget."

Some clients, when we ask what they have done in an attempt to overcome their problem, will say they have been to therapy. Usually (as in the case in Chapter Five), we will ask what the therapists did or suggested in regard to their problem. This gives a fuller and clearer picture of the attempts at solution. Here, the therapist failed to do that.

THERAPIST: So you did not do what the typical person does, which is to put too many things on your list so that there is no way you could get to them all?

KIRK: Just a little bit. It helped me to get more focused. But even there *(Laughs)*, I tended to list the junk mail in front of the biology. Or, I would put on the biology and not get to it. I have only written one paper since I graduated, and I am very creative in terms of the ideas I can come up with, so I feel quite frustrated. I feel like there is a part of me who does not want to do it. There is a part of me who wants to do it and another part of me which seems very resistant to it all.

THERAPIST: So you have tried different kinds of therapy and making lists. Anything else?

KIRK: I think what helps a little, sometimes, is to remember I am going to die, and my time is limited. That seems to get me going. People have also suggested that I was productive during grad school and did my job, and when I am in a situation when I have to do it, I get better. This is very true. When it has to be done, I am still OC, but I manage to do it.

THERAPIST: If I had a videotape in your house, what would I see?

KIRK: I would go to a reservoir where I would take some work with me. I would jog for an hour and fifteen minutes, go to the car, pick up the bag of mail or newspaper and go up to a nice naturey spot and just read the pile of junk mail or newspaper or maybe even a book that is not the main issue. Mainly the mail.

I would do this for three or four hours; I would be completely forgetting my goal, go home and eat a long, drawn-out dinner and watch TV, not in a compulsive TV way; something like NOVA or some science or nature show and then read some more junk mail, talk to my girlfriend, brush my teeth and maybe urinate and not be satisfied that it was a complete urination and spend five minutes making sure of that, all the time forgetting my goal and then, at the end of the day, chastising myself or reminding myself or vowing that tomorrow will be different.

THERAPIST: Not getting to your research and your writing seems to be a combination of at least two things: the things you are compelled to do like the junk mail plus other things you enjoy doing and you prefer doing rather than doing the research.

The therapist had sufficient information regarding the attempted solution; mainly, it was an injunction that "I must get on with the work!" It was put in many different ways, but they were all variations on that theme: setting deadlines, creating schedules, making to-do lists, seeking inspiration from meditation and hypnosis, and making promises that "tomorrow will be different." Friends had offered similar variations: "When you were in grad school, you did it. When it needs to be done, you can do it!"

With this in mind, the therapist framed the client's activities as a conflict between spending time on things he would *prefer* in contrast to that which he needed to do. In problems like Kirk's, no matter how needful the task, it is often tedious or laborious and is not inviting, akin to more common tasks such as bill paying, answering letters, studying for school, and housecleaning. In our experience, it is usually this uninviting aspect of tasks that is the barrier for many people.

Kirk's attempt at solution was fairly common. The client tries to overcome the barrier by pushing himself, at the same time "waiting for inspiration" to tackle the job, trying to get himself to a point of *feeling* like doing it. (One of the authors, R.F., once asked a friend, a television writer, how he was able to be inspired to turn out successful scripts week after week. His friend said, "Inspiration has nothing to do with it. Every morning, I drag myself from the breakfast table to my typewriter and sit down. That's the toughest part of it. Once I sit down, there's not much else to do but start writing. If you have any talent, you turn out a good script. If you don't have talent, you should get out of the field. The amazing thing is that following a day when I've written a lot and well, hardly thrown out any pages, the next morning, getting to the typewriter is still the same struggle. You know, I think that what's called 'writer's block' is the failure of the writer to deal with that initial wall of getting to the typewriter and sitting down.")

Sessions Two Through Seven

The remainder of the therapy pursued the strategy of interdicting Kirk's attempted solution by substituting restraining, the apparent blocking of his efforts to get on with his research.

The therapist was keeping in mind the danger of urging or encouraging Kirk's efforts to get on with it, as this would simply, and counterproductively, reinforce what had already been tried and had failed. The simplest way to avoid this mistake was instead to take a restraining stance. Thus, in the second session, the therapist suggested that there could be disadvantages to "getting on with it" and that these should be explored before arriving at any plan to tackle the problem in a different way.

After the third session, when Kirk was showing impatience and an eagerness to resolve the problem, the therapist offered a "compromise." Kirk would be "allowed" to do some work, but only at a very slow pace. Specifically, the therapist instructed Kirk that he was to sit down where he usually would do the work, note the time he sat down, and after *no more* than a half hour, he was to stand up and *not touch the work* for the rest of the day. In addition, he was to do this *only* twice a week.

In the fourth session, Kirk said that he was following the schedule but found ways to "cheat" and do more work beyond the half-hour limit. The therapist expressed concern that he was moving too fast and said that it was important to slow the work down. Kirk asked if the time limit could be extended even just ten or fifteen minutes longer. The therapist was firm that the half-hour limit should be kept and also made the next appointment three weeks hence.

By the fifth session, Kirk reported that he had worked a half hour every day during the preceding three weeks. He added that he found it difficult to stop but managed to maintain the half-hour limit. He was doing a lot more reading and some writing. This prompted the therapist to remind him of the disadvantages of improving.

In the seventh session, Kirk said he was finding it easier to maintain the pace of the reading and writing and that he was using his time more efficiently "because it is more of a habit." Again, the therapist cautioned him that he should improve slowly.

Follow-Up

In the follow-up three months after his last session, Kirk said he was less concerned about his productivity. He was continuing to work on his research for a half hour each day.

In the second follow-up, one year after the last session, Kirk was sustaining the change and doing more writing and had had one paper published.

7

Multiple Problems

Therapists can be discouraged when presented with a client who is expressing multiple problems, all of which seem serious and "chronic." The therapist will likely feel even more pessimistic if the client is socioeconomically disadvantaged. Contemporary psychotherapy still reflects the traditions of insight-oriented models. Working insightfully requires that the client be verbally adept and accustomed to dealing with abstractions. And because psychotherapy has been and to some extent still is lengthy, it also requires that clients be able to afford a rather expensive venture. "Poor folks" with little education have been regarded as unlikely candidates for psychotherapy. This unlikelihood has been attributed to limitations of the client rather than to those of the psychotherapeutic approach.

You are likely to be familiar with the label "multiproblem family." This label connotes that such a family is somehow fundamentally different from a family in which a member or members are simply having a problem. The differentness implies, among other things, that the family members are limited in their intellectual and motivational resources, that somehow they are enmeshed in a tangle of dysfunction, a mess. In our view, whether we are dealing with a family or an individual, we do not consider the situation different; rather, the clients simply have more than one problem.

We believe that pursuing one problem, the most disruptive for the individual, will relieve her of a disproportionate amount of distress while, at the same time, increasing the potential for improvement in another of her problems. One has to resist the temptation to decide for the client which problem should be "fixed" first. It is the client's values and priorities that we regard as important.

JUNE

This case illustrates the utility of focusing on the *main* problem while demystifying the pessimistic jargon so common in psychological labeling. We chose to present this case for two reasons. First, the client presented multiple complaints that had kept her in a chronic state of social isolation and poverty: depression, phobia, and a previous history of substance abuse. In the recent past, she had spent several years in jail. For many therapists, this picture is a discouraging one. Second, the therapist in this case was not one of the authors and at the time was one of the newer members of the Brief Therapy Center. To say the least, the case was a challenge for her. (As with all clients seen at the Center, colleagues may phone in comments or questions to the therapist; in the dialogues that follow, phone calls are labeled "BTC team.")

Session One

June was a fifty-three-year-old unemployed woman separated for many years from her husband. She lived with her thirty-year-old daughter in the daughter's house. June survived marginally by selling crafts, but as you will see, even this had become problematic for her.

> THERAPIST: What's the difficulty, the problem that brought you here today?
>
> JUNE: *(Long pause)* A whole bunch. I am depressed, and I have intense fears. I really have to stay on top of myself. I really

have to stay on top of my head because it gets overwhelming. Like my mail; I'm scared to open my mail. I am unemployed; I have no money.

THERAPIST: So, in your mail there could be bills? Is that what you are saying?

JUNE: Right! Right! I have an intense fear of anything you are supposed to take care of.

THERAPIST: That sounds rather reasonable to have those fears.

This comment is an example of normalizing—that is, framing the client's experience, albeit undesirable, as still within the normal range of human reaction. It's an implicit way of conveying, "OK, you have those fears, but there's nothing wrong with you in having them." Normalizing can engender in the client a sense of hopefulness in dealing with her troubles and, in turn, allow her to decrease the intensity with which she has been pursuing her attempted solution.

JUNE: They are very overwhelming. Like intense anxiety. I have to prepare myself for two weeks before I go get the mail because I can only get myself to get it once a month. That is a sample of . . . my previous experience of counseling was a positive one, so I did not have a fear, anxiety, at the anticipation of being on time and so on. I try to be punctual because I am very dysfunctional. I take many hours to do something.

THERAPIST: So, how did you get yourself to come here today?

Simply by raising that question, the therapist implied that although the client was defining herself as dysfunctional, she was nevertheless capable of overcoming it, of being capable of taking an action; this is another example of using implication to engender optimism in the client.

JUNE: Because I prepared my head. I cannot just do the things that I normally used to do. I have to prepare my head to do them so that the fear will not overcome me on something.

THERAPIST: And how do you prepare your head?

JUNE: Think it through as much as I can to make things as easy as I can. I eat up time. The reason I eat up time is I was in jail for a year. You learn to eat up time!

THERAPIST: What were you in jail for?

JUNE: Selling marijuana. I knew it was going to take me that long to get myself together again, and my husband was not able to hang in there and help me through that period. He left. I told him there was something and what could we do. He did not say anything. We went to bed, and he turned his back to me. I said I was going to go out for a drive and would be back soon.

When I came back, he wasn't there, and I have never seen him again. That was five years ago. I taught myself to use a computer while in jail. I took advantage of the situation. I spent a lot of time on the computer then, but I don't have one now. I did have a job for three years after I got out of jail, but now I'm unemployed, and I don't know how or where to find the rules.

It has been seven years, and I have lost my confidence. I pick up on people's vibes, and I am not sure what I am picking up, so I get afraid and cannot ask people what is wrong; it is uncomfortable. That is how I became unemployed just before we separated.

BTC TEAM: The first order of business is to identify the problem. She started out saying that she had severe fears, was depressed, and now is talking about jail, employment, her husband. Since it is important to focus on what we will be working on here, she started out by saying she had fears. Is that the main problem?

THERAPIST: We would like to find out what you would like to work on that is troublesome to you now.

JUNE: Fear of looking for employment. If I can get something, then I will feel secure and the fears will go away, I think. I am in another step of changing in my life. I have already done four of them but now I have another one and I feel I could go any way. How . . . what do I do?

THERAPIST: And it's a change from what to what?

In hindsight, it would have been better for the therapist to stick to the tangible agenda the client has mentioned, her fear of looking for employment. Instead, she diverted to the more abstract area of "change in my life." Yet this serves as a good example of how difficult it can be to obtain a clear statement of the client's problem. Here, June stated her problem but immediately embellished it with inviting but tangential issues.

JUNE: . . . to where I want to be. So I can accomplish something and be totally mentally healthy.

THERAPIST: You are mentioning the fears and in particular the fear of change—

JUNE: But see, it took me six months to even realize that I was dealing with anxiety. I did not know how to identify it.

THERAPIST: Would you say that that is the main area?

JUNE: Yes; yes.

THERAPIST: So if I am understanding you correctly, the main area seems to be your anxiety.

JUNE: Yes.

THERAPIST: Anxiety is different for different people, and I am trying to understand what it is like for you. So, let me ask you, how is this anxiety a problem for you?

Feelings, such as anxiety, are abstractions and more difficult for a client to change than the tangible and concrete impact of feelings. Here, the therapist was attempting to translate the vagueness of "anxiety" to more workable concrete factors.

JUNE: Things I have to go through to, let's say, just to get ready to get here. With anxiety. Going to get my mail. My stomach, pins, fears, shakes, not thinking or thinking clearly, not turning everything into negatives. Everything goes with what I am identifying as anxiety.

THERAPIST: So . . . what are you mainly afraid of?

JUNE: People.

THERAPIST: Can you give me an instance?

JUNE: I have been burned by people. I don't trust. I don't want to put myself out there. Why should I go through that hurt if I don't have to! (Cries)

THERAPIST: So then you do what?

JUNE: What I am doing now; trying to make it so that nobody can hurt me. I don't want to meet people. I want to know how to move on without putting any trouble into my life. I could go either way, right now. I could go out and just push a cart down the street. I cannot survive on what I have now.

So I have a choice: I can either go out there and be pushing a cart, or I can go out there and I can fight for "I'm going to be happy," make money, and make myself secure. But I don't know how to do that. I'm not ready to do that. There is a lot of preparation for me to be able to do that.

THERAPIST: What, in your estimation, do you have to do to prepare yourself?

JUNE: Deal with the anxiety, my fear of people. I'm stuck. Even though I know you go out there, you take the newspaper, go through it, clips, job-finding courses. I know it in my head but cannot force myself to do it. I am not happy with my life.

THERAPIST: Are you saying that you would like to get a job but don't know how to do it?

JUNE: I don't know that I'm saying I need to get a job. I need to be mentally secure. It may not be a regular job. I always have things to work out for me if I am out and about, meeting people. Positive things come to me. I am on a negative now. I don't like it, but I don't know how to get myself back to a point of positive. My spark is gone. (*Cries again*)

THERAPIST: It must be very hard to get that spark going when you have had bad experiences.

JUNE: My husband came down with MS. I did what I needed to do. I am a spontaneous person. I would go out there and what I needed, came!

THERAPIST: How long has this negative spirit been with you now?

JUNE: Since I got out of jail, seven years ago. I have a plan which is to use my own business license to get money and if anybody wants references, they can ask other vendors. But I need clothes to do that, and I need to have the energy to put into it. I am also having trouble with my body. I have increased my size, my hair is falling out because of stress . . .

BTC TEAM: Are we clear, then, that her main problem is most importantly that she is not making a living? She mentioned a few things that are obstacles to making a living: not having the confidence to call people to use them as a reference, not having the proper clothes. Are those the things which stop her or are there other things, too?

THERAPIST: My colleagues are saying you mentioned some things which were an obstacle to making a living: not having the confidence to call people for a reference, not having the proper clothes. Are those things which stop you?

JUNE: Yes.

THERAPIST: We are not clear what you consider to be the main obstacle.

JUNE: Getting myself moving; getting the strength to go out there.

THERAPIST: Usually when one has a problem, even if it has many components, one has to start some place; right?

JUNE: Yes.

June and the therapist continued in a circular pattern: the therapist kept pressing for what specifically and mainly stopped June from pursuing employment, while June rejoindered with abstractions, generalities. The main theme of the pattern was, What stops you from seeking employment?—I am fearful—Tell me more about fears. This is an example of what we call "the therapist working too hard." As demonstrated in the dialogue, the therapist asks a question in order to clarify the problem, but the client skirts the question and then adds more vague data, which the therapist pursues.

In this case, observers finally called in suggesting a different tack, one of apparently discouraging "getting out there." Here the team was useful in breaking this nonproductive loop, but you can do it working alone, usually by first recognizing that you are working too hard and getting nowhere. This realization can make it easier to approach the task from a different perspective or tack.

THERAPIST: One of my colleagues is hung up because you say you need to get rid of the fears and anxiety, but what good would that do if you still do not have clothes and are spending all your energy just to survive.

JUNE: He is right! That is my question too! That is why I am here. (*Laughs*) Because it gives you the energy to get started.

THERAPIST: But how would you do it with no clothes?

JUNE: I would probably go ahead and start with what I have and see where I could go with it!

THERAPIST: So, are the clothes an excuse you give yourself?

JUNE: It's just something I would have to deal with that would be a hurdle. I just don't want to go out there and deal with the system.

THERAPIST: So, to get moving may mean that you have to deal with that system, but you don't want to do that?

JUNE: If I am strong enough, I can kick it! Go out there and find where I belong. With this negativity, I am not going to go anywhere.

THERAPIST: We have to stop now, but since this is a very difficult situation, we would like you to give some thought to what obstacle is the first one that you want to overcome on your way to changing this negative thinking. It would save time if you can think about that between now and the next session.

Because we attach importance to obtaining from the client a clear description of the problem, this was the central task in the first session. Obtaining it required the entire session, because the client tended to talk in terms of metaphors, abstractions, and qualifications. This behavior is very common, especially with clients who have had previous therapy. Although the general area of the problem seemed reasonably clear—a fear of facing those tasks necessary to obtain employment—June was still scattered and vague in her responses to questions that could break down the problem into tangible, workable elements, in contrast to her "Getting myself moving, getting the strength to go out there." She still saw the problem as one of not having the right or sufficient spirit: "If I am strong enough, I can kick it." Thus, the therapist ended the session with an assignment in hope that it would direct June to think in small but tangible steps.

Session Two

The therapist started right off picking up the previous homework assignment.

THERAPIST: Last time we were talking about the obstacles to your getting going, and I thought I gave you a homework assignment to think about which of those obstacles was the most pressing for you. Did you take the opportunity to think about it?

JUNE: Oh, yes! I thought a lot about it. There are a lot that I mentioned last time and are still there, but I can handle them. I know how to handle those. I was able to eliminate a lot of them. I came down to confidence, aging, and trust. These are things that are underlying that I have to work on or deal with some way.

THERAPIST: Confidence, aging, and trust. I assume they are related, how?

JUNE: I trust myself with my judgment.

THERAPIST: Aging?

JUNE: I have a lot of fears that are halting me. I am seeing things that bother me, and I want to hold on to the past. Time goes very fast, and I also see the whole computer thing happening. Also, my family's gone, so I don't have anybody. But I don't want to go back into memories because that is when I start getting down. The aging scares me. But if I could deal with the confidence and trust in myself, the aging thing would go away.

THERAPIST: Are you saying, then, that if you have to prioritize, the confidence-trust issue would be first because if you could do something about that, you could deal with the other by yourself? It would not feel as threatening.

JUNE: Correct.

Here, as before, the therapist made few declarative statements. Her comments were almost always put as questions, yet, at the same time, they refined and focused the problem. This checking with the client, step by step, avoids the time-consuming problem of the client's saying later in therapy, "But that's not the problem."

THERAPIST: In terms of the confidence and trust, how does that show up? When you don't have confidence.

JUNE: I don't go for things that I could get.

THERAPIST: Could you please give me an example?

JUNE: It's hard because I can only think about examples where I would have confidence. But I am functioning on five cylinders although I have a six-cylinder motor. But here is one. Last week when I was coming here, I was looking for the cross street. I crossed the next street and did not even notice that I had gone over the first one I was looking for. I am not thinking in broader terms; this is something that bothers me. I need to cover my own back especially if I am in a job. I have to figure out a way to build confidence in me. I am functioning only because I pay attention to what is around me.

BTC TEAM: Supposing this business of confidence were no longer a problem, it would then mean that in order to get a job it would mean you would have to *do* something. What would you have to be doing that would ultimately, one would hope, lead to employment? The idea of it is to move away from confidence as an abstraction. It's shifting away from "feeling OK before I do it" to "How do I go about doing it?"

THERAPIST: What would be the first step that would lead to employment?

JUNE: Get myself out of my four walls. Go by people and just smile again. React again. Be out. I have shut most everything out. In terms of a job, I know different vendors that I would have to give references to. I would probably go through different angles. Other than just talking about it, I would go to temp offices, build myself up.

THERAPIST: That would be different than work with the vendors.

JUNE: Right.

THERAPIST: What would be the first step toward the temp services?

JUNE: Walking. I have tried to get myself to walk more. I used to do it a lot and enjoyed it. My neighborhood is not safe to walk, so I drive most places now.

BTC TEAM: If she drove here, does that mean she has the option to either drive or walk if she has to get some place? If the answer is yes, as far as the very first step, you could walk *or* drive toward a temporary employment place. (*The therapist conveyed that message to June.*)

JUNE: Oh! That would be easy. Before I drove I would have to call all the temp agencies, ask what they have going, whether they have anything going where I fit into, with most benefits for me, probably make an appointment, go out and meet them . . .

June seemed to discount the idea that taking a first step could be driving or walking to a temp agency—"Oh! That would be easy"—but then lists several things that would be necessary beforehand. However, the therapist persisted in her efforts to convert the "mountainous" into an attainable step at a time.

THERAPIST: So the first step would be to pick up the phone book and look up the numbers.

JUNE: *(Laughs)* I have the numbers sitting on my desk already. I have done that.

THERAPIST: So, can I take it, then, that the next step would be to pick up the phone and dial the number?

JUNE: Right! And accept that it is not going to hurt me. *(Laughs)*

THERAPIST: Just don't do it in a lightning storm, that is all.

JUNE: I would have to call the people that I would be using as references when I fill out the applications. I would have to do that before.

THERAPIST: Would a temp agency require references?

JUNE: Oh, yes.

THERAPIST: So, the next step would be to call someone you know rather than calling a stranger down the block to say, "Would you be a reference for me?"

JUNE: Right.

THERAPIST: So, would the first step, then, be to pick up the phone to call such a person?

JUNE: Yes. That is what I have been thinking about this week. Whether I should send such a letter first to this someone across the bay. It costs as much as a long-distance call, so I would have to keep it short so it does not cost as much. If I did all the explaining in the letter I could do that. I could even ask them to give me a call.

THERAPIST: So the very first step would be to send that letter off.

JUNE: Yes. Even one good reference might be enough for something.

THERAPIST: Part of my thinking on this is that while you are working on your confidence, etc., it might hold you to go through some of the motions of going about seeking work. Taking small steps, even going through the motions. So that I would say that for the time being, go no further than writing the letter, but don't mail it. It is strictly for the purpose of getting the feeling of getting back into the swing of things.

JUNE: Gotcha!

THERAPIST: Like a dry run, so to speak. I think it is better to err on the side of moving too slowly than too quickly.

JUNE: OK. That really answers it. Because, you see, I got one reference, and then I thought, "I can't do it because I'm not ready to go out and do it." Now, this gives me a way. OK, gotcha! (*Smiles broadly*) That's what I'm going to do. Thank you, thank you!

When people are fearful of tackling a task (as in "phobic" states), or, similarly, when they are intimidated by the enormity or tedium of it (as in "procrastination") the most commonly reported attempt at dealing with their problem is to "wait until I feel ready to tackle it. I'm not ready right now; this is not a good time." We refer to this as waiting for inspiration (as we saw in the case of Kirk in Chapter Six). We see the *getting started*, taking the first step, as the strategic hurdle, and, once someone has started, we anticipate that the continuation of the effort will ensue automatically. Thus, one way or another, we direct the clients to taking that first step, while at the same time making that first step as achievable as possible. As we saw in the preceding dialogue, this often takes the form of leading the client to the first step but then limiting any further effort: "Sit down and write the letter *but don't mail it*." In this session, the therapist was able to help June define obstacles as small, concrete tasks and to offer a tangible step toward dealing with those tasks.

Session Three

Ordinarily, when a therapist has given the client some homework, checking on it is the first order of business for the ensuing session. However, on the way into the therapy room, June had said something to the therapist that indicated some change in her problem. A change in the problem always takes highest priority, and the therapist inquired about it straightaway.

> THERAPIST: On your way in, you were saying that you were doing much better. Could you tell us about it? What's been going on in the last week?
>
> JUNE: Nothing has been going on except my thinking. OK; I was to write a letter when I left here, sometime during the week, which was no problem. Took care of that.
>
> THERAPIST: You did?

We prefer to convey approval by an expression of surprise rather than by the more conventional means of giving explicit praise. Using the latter form runs the risk of being heard or sensed by the client as condescension, a one-up position of patting the client on the head. Our preferred form defines the client as being ahead of the therapist, thus allowing the client to feel one-up. It also implies that the client made a significant step.

> JUNE: But as I did, I realized that, like I have been saying, I know how to do these things, so why aren't I moving?
>
> THERAPIST: How were you able to get yourself moving to write the letter?
>
> JUNE: Well, I had a goal to do, so I did it. But I have had other goals before and it just wasn't happening; why?
>
> THERAPIST: So, how did you do it?

JUNE: Oh, just right after I left. What I came to is . . . why am I not doing what I know I have to do to get myself going?

THERAPIST: Let me come back a little because I am confused. You left here. You went home, sat down, and wrote the letter?

JUNE: Right. How easy it was to write the letter. Why can I not go on with other things that I need to do to move forward?

BTC TEAM: This time she wrote the letter. But she says that she has set goals for herself in the past and not gone through with it. The question, then, is what was different this time that she went ahead with it.

The purpose of this message is to have the client shift her focus from "Why *can't* I?" to "What do I do so that I *can?*" It also encourages a shift from Why to What.

THERAPIST: My colleagues were interested in how you were able to do it this time.

JUNE: Probably because I had made a commitment here. I am that kind of person. I follow through with commitments. It is part of what I like about me. I follow up and do not leave people hanging. What I realized on the way here is that I have put up a self-defense layer because of something that was going on in my life. Now I have to start putting it down. The first thing was doing something which is me: sitting down and writing a note to someone is part of who I am. But it was hard to do initially. So, a lot of the positive things about me that I like, I can put back in me, which will make me become whole again.

THERAPIST: Is that the difference with the other times when you don't do what you know you need to? You went home from here, and you wrote the letter without thinking too much, and with the things that you do not get done, you do a lot of thinking?

JUNE: Yes, that is the difference. I wrote the letter without thinking about all of the other things I am scared about and so on. It was all in one thing. While I was thinking in my head what I was going to tell her in the letter, I started thinking that I need to make myself more solid again. When I can do that, things just sort of come my way. I can go for it.

THERAPIST: You go for it, so things come.

JUNE: Yeah. I just go out there, ask questions, check things out, and normally what I need just comes to me. But you have to be confident to do this. It is time to shed the cover and go for it. I got to.

THERAPIST: That seems to be the case except you can bring yourself down by ruminating on everything that can go wrong.

JUNE: Yes. The only way that I am going to sell myself to a potential job is by feeling positive about myself. I have to shake the blues and feel more positive, good about me. When I came here, I was on the verge of sleeping four days straight, from Sunday through Thursday. Now, I am working on getting out of the depression mode by Monday afternoon, which is by getting a regular amount of change. Before, I was scaring myself to death; now, I am doing something different.

THERAPIST: That sounds like very rapid change. I am a little concerned. You said that you were sleeping four days and you say now you are just sleeping one and a half days?

JUNE: Right. Because I have something else going now. I started moving, going places. Like tonight. I have a place I can go, possibly where I can make some money.

THERAPIST: You do? What is that?

JUNE: There is a show in town which is no longer a new show so I am not going to get burned.

THERAPIST: How did you get yourself to go out and find out about this show and get yourself in it?

June had presented us with a remarkable improvement: rather than spend the bulk of her week sleeping hoping to feel strong enough to face the world of work, she had decided to take some action by getting out of her house. In the next dialogue, she describes how that step led to another so that she was now in a position to earn some money. This kind of report can tempt a therapist to encourage the client to take another step, or at least to cheer the client on: "See, you can do it!" But that would be a reversal of the strategy that had worked: breaking tasks down into small, manageable steps and then posing some restraint in moving on. Equally, we hope to convey that the accomplishment is hers, not ours. Thus, the therapist here was not ignoring what we considered a significant step the client had taken but was acknowledging it in a way different than is conventionally taken.

The therapist, therefore, persisted with the focus on what the client was *able* to *do,* usually put in the form of a question. Buried in that question was the presumption that the client actively and purposively *did* something, some heretofore impossible task. Thus, the therapist confirmed the client's capability implicitly rather than explicitly.

> JUNE: Well, I was out surviving and I ran into somebody that I had not seen in about eight years. We started talking, and she told me about this show. This is how things usually happen for me. I am out there—
>
> THERAPIST: How were you able to get yourself out there and circulate in a different area?
>
> JUNE: I took a gamble. A place invited me to sell where I had sold before, and I said yes. I have to make money, and this may happen one in fifty times that I go out.
>
> THERAPIST: It may happen only one in fifty times, but if you did not go out there, it would happen zero times.

This comment echoes the thought that achievement can come about with one small step.

> JUNE: Right, right! That is why I want me out there. (*Smiles broadly*) The more I like me, the more I know I am not

going to lose a thing going out there! Because I do it right. I was, for the first time, stopping and utilizing the skills that I know this head has.

THERAPIST: So you are saying that not only were you out there but you were thinking differently about how you were going to approach things so that they would turn out better?

JUNE: Yeah. I did think about how to make things happen.

THERAPIST: It sounds like you took a very active role in asking this person, "Where are there shows I can go to?" and then you got some information.

JUNE: Yes.

The therapist decided to close the session by offering June some homework.

THERAPIST: What would be the equivalent of the letter this week? Something small, please.

JUNE: To finish my calendar for the next eight months.

THERAPIST: That is too big.

JUNE: No, no. I have it in my head already. It would take me half an hour to do it.

THERAPIST: Which half hour? This afternoon or tonight?

JUNE: Not today because I have to put energy into making money tonight. But tomorrow, yes.

THERAPIST: At about what time?

JUNE: At two P.M.

THERAPIST: Please, would you be willing to promise us and yourself that tomorrow at two P.M. you will sit down in front of your calendar, and when two-thirty comes around you finish, no matter how much or how little you have accomplished? You work no longer.

JUNE: Yes.

THERAPIST: Thank you. We'll see you next week at the same time.

Here again is another example of setting the client at the task but then restraining her. It is a form of getting the client to depart from the common practice of trying to push ahead but in the face of fear. Instead, the client overcomes the barrier of the fear because the task is limited to a small step. Once having taken the first step, the client either anticipates taking a second step the next day or perhaps "disobeys" the therapist by moving ahead beyond the restraint herself. In either case, the forward momentum becomes the client's.

Ordinarily, when a client returns and reports a significant improvement, we terminate that session by using restraint in a different way. We take the position that the improvement they made went beyond what we had expected; and, because of that, we define the change as improving too fast. We might say, "It's better to improve too slowly than too quickly." On that premise, we end the session urging that the client do nothing to improve further "at least until we meet again." We might add that we would feel even more comfortable if the client would do her best to bring about some relapse "because you have moved so fast." Occasionally, we might schedule the next appointment for two weeks ahead rather than take the customary one-week hiatus. We'll explain that meeting too soon runs the risk of too rapid further improvement. Consistent with that framing, we do not assign any task or homework that would indicate how to make further advances.

If you examine what would otherwise seem as a discouraging direction, you might see that there are a number of beneficial implications in it. First, we are conveying that definite improvement has taken place. Second, we are establishing that the improvement is the client's own doing, not ours. Third, we are conveying that the client is on an inevitable upward course, one that will require effort to slow down; associated with that, the client has control of making things better (otherwise why plead that she not do anything to improve further?). Finally, it is a no-lose arrangement for the client.

We anticipate that in any case, improvement may not take a smooth and continuously upward course. We don't want clients to feel they have failed if they return and say that things have not improved further or have even gotten worse. This risk is all the greater if the client feels she wants to please the therapist with continuing good news. The therapist's framing saves the client from this risk; there is no way for her to lose. Whether her report is "no further change" or "things have gotten worse," she has *succeeded* in complying with the therapist's plea. If, instead, the client reports further improvement, the relief from her problem offsets the therapist's "disappointment." As you might expect, we do not say "Great" but, rather, express our concern for her having moved too fast yet again, and we urge her more strongly to delay any further improvement.

Session Four

As we said earlier, although there can be exceptions, when a therapist has given the client some homework in the previous session, she will start the next session by checking on that homework, mainly to see if the client has complied with it, *how* she has done it, and what, if anything, has come of it. In this session, the therapist started a bit too generally but, fortunately, the client interpreted it as asking about the assignment.

> THERAPIST: How have things been in the last week?
>
> JUNE: Well, I did what I was supposed to do. The next day between two and two-thirty, I sat down and finished my calendar, which I had already thought about so I basically had it done; so, I have that taken care of. I also made a few calls, just to—
>
> THERAPIST: You sat down between two and two-thirty, and what did you do during that time?
>
> JUNE: OK. Opened my calendar, looked up my open dates. I had curiosity about some things that I had flyers on but did not know that much about, so I called a couple of them.

THERAPIST: All of that in a half hour?

JUNE: Yes, 'cause I already had it in my head. That is it! That is the thing. I can have it in my head, but I don't do it!

THERAPIST: So, how did you get yourself to do it?

JUNE: Because I said I would do it!

THERAPIST: As easy as that?

JUNE: Yes. It would not have been so easy if I had had no idea as to where to start with it. But I already had it in my head. It was just doing it.

THERAPIST: From what I have understood, when we were talking about difficulties of getting going, it sounded to me like maybe some times you know what you need to do, but you have difficulty doing it. So, I am wondering how the hell you got yourself to do it!

JUNE: I made a commitment here, so I did it! And then, also when I left here, I was going to try out a new place, so I went on Wednesday night; money was not that great but the positive influences were.

THERAPIST: A new place selling your crafts?

JUNE: Right. But the positive reinforcement I got—

THERAPIST: In what way?

JUNE: Just by what the people were saying. "It's great!" "You have to come back!" "I don't have money now. How can I get a hold of you?" That was the starting of it, and then I went out Saturday and Sunday, which are my normals. Nothing different; same places I would have gone last month or this month, and the feedback was different.

THERAPIST: How so?

JUNE: Positive.

THERAPIST: What were they saying?

JUNE: "If I want to buy a lot, can I get hold of you? May I have your card?" I looked . . . what is the difference? What is the difference? I noticed I was smiling, with my eyes as well as my mouth. Whenever I went out to a grocery store, just running in and out, it was different. Like I said, I was trying to figure out what was different. All I could come up with was that my eyes were smiling, my whole body was smiling, not just my face.

THERAPIST: And how did you get your whole body smiling?

JUNE: Coming here. Being able to put a few things in line; feeling like I am moving ahead. Things going positive for me on the weekend. Somebody came to talk to me about a problem they were having, being unemployed. She has a lead on a thing; she is going to do it and check it out and feed back to me; let me know whether there is a possibility that I could fit into what I am doing. This would be a job situation. That, in turn . . . that sort of just came. It was somebody I had not talked to in years but all of a sudden . . .

THERAPIST: So how did you talk to this person?

JUNE: She came over and started talking with me.

THERAPIST: Oh. You mean she had not talked to you before, and this time she did?

JUNE: Just a "Hi." And all of a sudden she started telling me her situation.

THERAPIST: Were you aware of what you were doing differently in that situation?

JUNE: No. Except for my eyes smiling. A guy that I was beside two months ago, I thought my behavior was the same, and I was kind of shocked that he came over and he told me his name, who he was. . . . Usually, you say good-bye to whoever is set up next to you; this time, he introduced himself, gave me clue on where to go. "This is something I can give you," he said. He gave me a situation that I could possibly do something with on selling.

And, like I say, I thought I was being open all the time. But a lot of times I am thinking I am open, and I must be giving a closed message, even though I think I am not. I must be because—

THERAPIST: I guess it would be really useful to know what it is that you are doing now that gives an open message.

JUNE: Right! The only thing I could come down with was, my eyes are smiling. They looked happy. And that comes from growing 'cause I am a person who needs to grow, moving, doing things. Otherwise I stagnate; I become depressed, unhappy.

THERAPIST: What do you think you were doing that made you grow in this situation?

As you may notice, June tended to lapse into "feeling right" as the key to getting out of her morass and achieving success. This is a common notion, that one must first *feel* right (confident or unafraid or optimistic) *before* one can act. Spontaneously evoking a "right" feeling is usually not feasible, but taking an action is more accessible, and it is the taking of an action and the results it brings that achieve a "right" feeling. In general, tackling a task is more likely to inspire a person's confidence than trying to be confident so that she can tackle the task. The therapist persisted with "What do you *do* . . . ?" putting the focus on *action*.

JUNE: I guess, just doing something. Achieving something.

THERAPIST: Uh huh.

The therapist did not question that response. Instead she gave an implicit confirmation.

JUNE: Like I know from now until the end of the year, what moves I can make. I checked out possible options. I know I have the bases covered. Now, I just need to keep my eyes open, see if I can find a better situation to move into than what I already have.

THERAPIST: You know, when you begin to make progress, it is always dangerous to become too optimistic.

JUNE: Oh, yes! It kind of scares me right now.

THERAPIST: And because progress never occurs in a straight line up. It is more like two steps forward and a half-step back. I would caution you that this is going to be it. I would feel more comfortable if you could almost count on there being a relapse at some point. You've been going up for some time now.

As we have described elsewhere, this kind of statement is our more usual way of responding to a report of improvement. The remainder of the session was spent in talking about what a relapse would look like. When June expressed discomfort at the prospect of a relapse, the therapist, rather than reassure her it is not likely to happen, instead urged her to *plan* a relapse. "It's a very useful way to put on the brakes when progress has occurred so fast."

At first glance, it would seem that the therapist was being very discouraging, very "negative," and that this would diminish the client's confidence. However, you may notice that the language used did not convey a *warning* about a relapse but anticipated one and characterized its occurrence as normal. The therapist strengthened this idea by *recommending* a relapse, one that the client should plan.

We often schedule a subsequent session for two or more weeks later. "OK; let's meet again next week," can trivialize improvement. In this case, the next appointment was held three weeks later.

Session Five

As we've said, checking on homework is usually the first order of business. However, when the assignment has to do with possible change in the problem, we are not looking for compliance with a task but whether there has been any further improvement.

THERAPIST: In our last session I had asked you to hold off on making any further improvement. I was wondering if you were able to do that.

The therapist's phrasing (framing) was deliberate. She did not ask if there had been further improvement or not. Instead, she reminded June that she had asked her to "hold off" making any further improvement and wondered if she had "been *able to do that*." Both comments implied that the client had control over her problem. It was also a no-lose framing, because if the client reported she hadn't made any further progress, she had succeeded with the therapist's request. However, if she should report that she had made further progress, her satisfaction with the situation would be likely to eliminate the idea that she had "failed" the assignment.

> JUNE: No. (*Laughs*) Things just happened.
>
> THERAPIST: What happened?
>
> JUNE: When I came in here, I had no hope, no dreams. I could not, I was not able to. That was one of the reasons I was here. And by coming to sessions here, I have gotten some of that back. I am more outgoing now, which is one of the things I was trying to achieve. I went through quite a few tight situations and dealt with them and, in turn, that brought about the improvement that I was wanting.

Session Six

In the sixth session, June reported further progress: she had gotten more work and had started exercising, something that had been a concern of hers for quite some time. The therapy was terminated at that sixth session; the remaining four sessions would be held for her in the bank should she feel the need to come back.

Because the strategy of "go slowly in making any further improvement" did no harm and likely enhanced or solidified change, the therapist's closing note was to caution June against making "too much" progress "too quickly." (Both phrases are so vague that they allow the client to define them any way she wants.)

Follow-Up

In the follow-up done ten months after her last appointment, June said she had gotten "a few more things going." She was doing alterations in her home for a dry-cleaning firm, but she was still afraid of going out, afraid of people.

"I've done good. I'm bringing in some money; I cold-called the dry-cleaners," but she was still afraid to deal with the customary job search task. She felt it necessary to track down her ex-husband and reinsure her car; she accomplished those tasks. She added that she was still trying to figure herself out, and she monitored herself. For example, she realized that when she was occupied, she didn't cry even at the memory of her mother's or daughter's deaths. Finally, she said that she had not sought any further therapy.

When we evaluate outcomes of therapy, there is often a pull between using measures consistent with more traditional models, in which normative factors are considered important (i.e., a deviation from "normal" behavior), and working from our model, which is non-normative. Our model is complaint-based, and as such there is no meaningful concept of normal or abnormal.

In this case, June reported that she was still afraid of going out and afraid of people. However, we don't know whether this constituted a problem for her. It would have been better to have asked her explicitly at the follow-up rather than to have relied on the fact that she had not sought further therapy. Her stated fears are a little contradictory, for example, her main means of exercise was walking, yet this required going out; to arrange for work in her home also required contact with people, especially when it involved "cold" contact as she described. It would have been useful to have asked her to clarify these contradictions, as it would have made clearer the degree of resolution of her original complaints.

Seriousness can be defined in many ways. We usually think of the obvious: suicide, homicide, self-starvation come to mind. The following case presents a problem that if unresolved could wreck the career of the client and, likely, her whole social future. Although this outcome lacks the drama of suicide, for example, in our minds it is nevertheless a serious problem. This kind of case is also intimidating to many therapists not only because of the medical complications that can ensue but also because the behavior of the client invites discouraging diagnoses, such as psychosis.

8

I Can't Stop Mutilating Myself

A therapist can identify more easily with those problems that we might consider the everyday variety, problems that are simply excesses of normal activities or functions, such as insomnia, marital conflict, child-rearing difficulties, phobias, and obsessions. But problems that go beyond or outside the range of usual human activity are much less easy to identify with and are considered bizarre. Attributing bizarreness to problems will tend to make those problems more difficult to resolve; it is not unusual for therapists to rely on referral to a psychiatrist and medication. Self-mutilation, the compulsion to repeatedly injure and scar oneself, is one of these problems.

LAURA

Laura was a twenty-four-year-old graduate student committed to pursuing a professional career. She was preparing for her career at a university that had very high standards; she was also holding a part-time position in a firm related to that career. The job itself also was demanding, and both areas together produced enormous and continuing stress for her. An additional stress for her was that her chosen career as well as her hopes for a good social life required a presentable appearance. Her difficulty in this latter area was what eventually led her to seek help.

Session One

The therapist began with the same question we ask in every case.

THERAPIST: What is the problem? What is the concern that brings you in here today?

LAURA: For the last few years I've had a really bad problem with my skin. I have a residual acne from when I was a teenager, like many people have. I don't really have a very serious problem with acne except I have a really severe compulsive behavior about scratching my skin, picking at it, ripping at it, and then when it starts to heal, picking the scabs off. I constantly have scabs and infections from me putting my fingers in it, playing with it, manipulating the blemishes. It is so distracting and hard for me to concentrate sometimes that I spend hours, like in my bathroom, picking at my skin, and I make it really bad. Sometimes I make it bleed and get it quite swollen, and my dermatologist yells at me all the time and tells me not to do it, but I just don't seem to be able not to do it.

THERAPIST: You say, bear with me because I am very concrete, that you spend hours. Is it literally hours or a few minutes here and there?

LAURA: It is literally sometimes hours. Not really more than two. And it is sometimes broken up. Like I'll sit down and read a book for five minutes—

THERAPIST: At home? Not at work?

LAURA: At home. There is a little bit of a social shame element involved in doing it. When I am out in public. But when I am at home and I need to study and I have a lot of work to do, I cannot focus on anything except running to the bathroom every few minutes to see if I am breaking out; how it looks. Is it more red or more swollen than it was before? And then when I finally stop touching, it is so red and swollen that I cannot go outside my apartment looking like that. Then I end up with hydrocortisone and all these anti-inflammatory lotions.

THERAPIST: You call your dermatologist?

LAURA: No, no! I don't ever admit to him that I do it. I tell him that I am over it, I don't do it anymore, but of course, when he looks at my skin, it has been picked at, so I keep ice in my freezer all the time and cortisone lotions which I keep having refilled. It goes sort of in phases. There are some times when it is not so bad, but then it seems to always flare up again and gets really bad. Unfortunately I do a lot of damage to my skin, and even if I feel like that for one day, I can basically infect my skin so badly that it takes weeks for it to heal back up. So then I have to live with a very disfigured face for a long time. It's having a really bad impact on my social life and on my ability to really study and devote a lot of attention to being in school and going out with friends. I am so worried with this problem.

THERAPIST: Are you aware of what happens just before you go and pick your face?

LAURA: Uh huh. This last time it happened, I cannot remember exactly what I was thinking about. I remember that I was in a good mood and was getting ready for bed. I was going to wash my face and do those sorts of things. When I looked in the bathroom mirror I thought, oh, I look tired and my skin looks kind of flaky, 'cause I use a drying lotion, like gel, so sometimes it looks like skin that is peeling off. And I remember I started to scratch at the dead skin that was peeling anyway and then I started to think of, I think I'm starting to break out here in my chin; something like that, and then it sort of escalated really quickly into a frenzy of being really worried about how I look.

THERAPIST: So you were not going to the bathroom to pick your face, which, I take it, sometimes you do?

LAURA: Yes, sometimes I do.

THERAPIST: What is an example of when you go into the bathroom with the intention of picking your face?

LAURA: It seems like it usually happens when I am doing something else and I like rest my face against my hands, and I feel some kind of bump or blemish and I become obsessed with seeing what it looks like, how big it is, and become very upset that it's there. And I am very sensitive about my skin. I always feel like it is tingling or breaking out.

THERAPIST: You have become an expert.

LAURA: So, if that happens I can no longer do what I was doing—reading or whatever I was doing. No matter where I am, if it is in the library or something, I have to run up and go to the ladies' room. But the lighting in there is really bad, so I don't usually pick because I cannot see.

THERAPIST: You said that there are times when you do less picking. How come?

LAURA: I guess when things are really terrible in my life. I am really busy. I run from class to class, to work, to do homework, to a library, to a study group, and I am so frantically busy that I am just too distracted to think about myself. And sometimes when things are really going badly or are very stressful, I am really preoccupied with some other problem; I don't worry. But as soon as I have time to take a breath or have enough leisure time, it becomes all-consuming.

THERAPIST: What made you pick up the phone and call us now as opposed to a week ago or a month ago?

The question "Why now?" is one we usually ask clients once they have described their complaint. It has several uses. First, we always want to confirm whether the client is seeking us out for the purpose of getting some help—is the complainant or voluntary client—or whether the client is not there seeking help but has come at the behest or coercion of someone else and therefore is an involuntary client.

The question "Why now?" can elicit that information in the early phase of therapy. A response detailing how the problem has become intolerable for the client, has come to affect her life in a quantitatively painful way, reflects a voluntary client. However, a response that someone else has urged the client to seek help at this time is more redolent of an involuntary client. We will usually follow up this latter response with the question, "If that person didn't suggest (urge, demand) you to come in, would you be here, at least at this time?" A no answer confirms that the client is coming in under duress.

In that case, we are unlikely to proceed by saying, "OK, let's get on with the therapy," because that would fly in the face of the client's position: "I am not here to undertake therapy." Laura might have said, for example, "Well, the problem hasn't bothered me that much, but my dermatologist said he wouldn't treat me anymore unless I sought help. That was last week, so I called you the next day."

However, Laura's response was as follows.

LAURA: Well, about a year ago it was so bad that I was having trouble even going to work because my skin was always swollen, red, and discolored. It would take me *hours* in the morning to get ready to go anywhere. I had to put ice on it to make the swelling go down enough. I looked like I had been in an accident or someone had hit me because it would be all bruised. It looked really bad, and people always asked me, "What happened to you?" and I became very self-conscious, so self-conscious that I would not want to go out like that and be seen.

So, at that point my life was falling apart, and I did not want to lose my job or anything, but I couldn't even focus, because of my skin, at work. So I decided to find help, and I was referred to an agency in the area. One problem that I have had in going to therapy is that finances are extremely limited. I have been having a lot of financial problems which got worse since I went back to school. But since I had to pay a very low fee I was finally able to get some therapy. My therapist there was trying really hard to work on the problem with me, but she tends to

think of it as symptomatic of other problems, so she's been trying to address those. We have talked through some things, and I
think it has helped me to cope better with some problems like
my family issues, but the fact is that I have continued this
behavior, though not as bad as it was; but at any rate, they had a
year-long limit and we are terminating next week, so she suggested that since this problem has not been taken care of enough
for me that I should pick up some other therapy.

THERAPIST: Let me switch gears a little and ask you something different. You have had this problem for a while, and you
probably have tried to do things in order to stop the scratching.
In order to save time, I would like to know what you have tried
in your best efforts to stop this problem that have not worked or
have not worked well enough, otherwise you wouldn't be here.

LAURA: I tried doing other things like taking walks, leaving my apartment or calling people on the phone to distract
myself. That didn't really work; I actually kept people on the
phone, long distance, while I went to the bathroom to pick and
then would come back.

THERAPIST: What would you tell them?

LAURA: "Hold on, the cat wants in," and then actually
leave the phone. I cannot believe I did this. This is like *long distance!* I also put newspapers all over the mirrors in my house so
that I could not see my reflection. I tried wearing gloves all the
time, even inside of the house, but that did not work. I could
not have my hands covered all the time because I cannot turn
pages in books and things like that. I tried watching TV or lis-
tening to music; that did not work.

THERAPIST: So it sounds like distraction does not work.

LAURA: Right. One thing that does help is physical exercise, mostly because it just makes me feel better; but this urge
comes over me at night, especially just before I go to bed. It is
not safe for me to walk around my neighborhood alone at night.
So I have not been able to explore that option in depth.

The therapist asked Laura what she had done in her efforts to resolve her problem—that is, what her attempted solution was. Laura mentioned a number of things that most people would regard as logical and appropriate, mainly to distract herself from the urge to pick at her face, but to no avail. And although exercise helped, Laura's access to exercise was limited, and, more important, the benefit was only temporary.

Under these circumstances, clients are apt to feel helpless in the face of what they experience as an overwhelming, unconquerable force. However, the therapist's comment, "It sounds like distraction doesn't work," implied that Laura had been depending on only one avenue of effort and further implied that some other avenue might work. This is an example of intervening by implying there are unexplored options, options that hold promise of change.

> THERAPIST: Anything else?
>
> LAURA: Drug therapy. My therapist is a social worker, so she referred me to an M.D. who prescribed like Valium for me, and it had absolutely no effect. I think that is about everything I have tried.
>
> THERAPIST: Let me go back to something I was not clear on. You seem to imply that there are different levels at which you pick your face.
>
> LAURA: Yes. There is drawing blood, and then there is picking just a little bit. (Laura makes gestures of lightly scratching her face.) Sometimes I have an appointment in two days, and I tell myself, "You really cannot do this."
>
> THERAPIST: And how does that work?
>
> LAURA: Sometimes it does because I feel so bad knowing that I am going to have to see people at a particular day and time. People ask me about it.
>
> THERAPIST: And you say . . . ?
>
> LAURA: Well, I have many answers that I have prepared. Sometimes I say that I was in an accident. Sometimes I say that

I have allergies or eczema. It does not look like normal acne, so telling people it is normal acne does not seem to satisfy them. They look at me even though that is the root problem for it.

THERAPIST: I presume there are other people who know about this problem. What have they advised you to do?

LAURA: They always tell me to just stop it. They presume it is just voluntary. Well, I suppose it is.

THERAPIST: And the therapist you have been working with, what has she said about it?

LAURA: We have not talked about it too much because, as I said, she thinks it has to do with deeper problems. So she says I should make other lifestyle changes. She has not addressed the issue of the particular moment, of when I have the urge to go do it. She thinks I need to get out more, to socialize more, not to be isolated. She thinks it has a lot to do with being bored.

THERAPIST: And the picking is limited to your face?

LAURA: Yes. I do not break out in other places.

THERAPIST: (A colleague in the observation room calls the therapist.) My colleagues say that it sounds like being out there, in public, with a bloody face must be pretty bad. They want to know what would be even worse? What could you do to yourself that would be worse?

LAURA: I don't know. I guess another thing that I worry about is my weight, and I guess if I gained a lot of weight. . . . That would be very embarrassing.

THERAPIST: OK. We are going to have to stop soon, so I would like to ask you to think about something until the next time we meet. What would be a small but significant change that would let you know that, even though you are not out of the woods with this problem, you are starting to move in the right direction? A small, concrete but significant change that would let you know that things were improving. It would not necessarily have to do with your face.

Simply asking people to give thought to signs of change, even a small change, can be a useful intervention. For if a client gives any thought to improvement, she has accepted the implicit premise that things can or will change; this in turn engenders a more hopeful outlook on the outcome of therapy. When people are more hopeful or optimistic, they may reduce the desperate efforts they have been making in struggling with the problem, which can lead to a change in the problem itself.

Session Two

As with most sessions in which suggestions and homework have been given in the previous session, we started session two by asking for the client's compliance. Here, we were interested in Laura's response to the implication that her problem could improve.

THERAPIST: We had asked you to think about something. Did you take the opportunity to do it?

LAURA: Yes. It was really hard for me to think in terms of something small. I really have a problem always being late because it takes me such a long time to cover up the blemishes and do what I need to do to get out the door. So I really think that if I could get through my morning routine and get up and be on time—whether or not my skin is broken out, to be able to leave the house on time and not keep coming back into the house and into the bathroom to keep adding stuff on my face. I think I would feel like I was willing to go out instead of trying to make everything look right. I cannot get out the door now. I find myself paralyzed by this skin problem.

I feel like I function less well under less pressure. I am more efficient, faster, when I am under lots and lots of pressure. It is very strange, and I do not want to live under stress. Once I have picked at my face, I feel so bad and embarrassed, I do not want to go out, and I feel like I have a reason not to see people. If my face is all broken out and swollen I can tell myself that today I will not see anybody because I look so terrible. If, on the other hand, I *decide* I will not see anyone, then I think I am antisocial and I feel terrible.

THERAPIST: *(Another call from colleagues in the observation room)* It makes a lot of sense that you are concerned with picking your face and, of course, related to that, concerned with your appearance. It is a very realistic concern, particularly in the professional field that you have chosen and because you are going to be in the public eye a lot. What my colleagues are asking is that, in terms of our next meeting, you think about this concern in depth. In thinking about it, you may want to choose one day in which you allow yourself to freely think about this concern more than the rest of the time and be concerned about your appearance and freely decide that you are going to pick on your face that day. You might want to do this in thinking about this realistic concern that you have. OK?

LAURA: What about the other days?

THERAPIST: Well, you are going to be thinking about this in general and freely pick a day in which you are going to be doing it in more depth.

LAURA: But I don't *have* to pick on my face.

THERAPIST: We want you to think about this very realistic concern of yours, and you may choose to pick on your face one day. Your friends are telling you and you sometimes tell yourself that this is not a big deal, and we disagree with this. It is a very legitimate concern.

Although the instruction to Laura may seem strange, it was strictly in keeping with our model. Because we view the client's attempted solution as the prime factor in maintaining the very problem she is trying to resolve, resolution requires a departure from that effort. Here, Laura clearly described her efforts, which, although all executed in different ways (scolding herself for picking, trying to distract herself from the urge to pick, being told "Just stop it!"), were variations of the theme "You must stop picking at your face!" Ergo, a clear departure from that "solution" would be, "You *must* pick at your face!" The particular way for her to implement this new injunction was to ask her to select a day when she would deliberately pick at her face.

Session Three

The suggestion given at the close of the previous session—for Laura to choose a day to pick at her face —was a central one, as it focused directly on her attempted solution to avoid this behavior. We were very interested in her response to this suggestion.

THERAPIST: We had asked you to do something last time. Did you take the opportunity to do it?

LAURA: Yes.

THERAPIST: How did it go?

LAURA: I think it helped a lot. You told me to choose a day that I could worry and freely pick at my skin, so I chose Monday since I hate Mondays anyway, *(Laughs)* and it really helped me all weekend not to pick at my skin much at all, because I said to myself that this was not my day to worry about it so don't even think about it, and it helped to take away the urge, the intense need to pick at it. On Monday, I really didn't even feel like picking at it very much, and I did some Monday night. Unfortunately it spilled over some into Tuesday, but I really felt like I had a boundary on it. It just helped.

THERAPIST: How about the two days prior to the weekend, since you left from here?

LAURA: I did not pick. I made Monday the day right away, so I did not pick. I did some but not to the extent that I would have otherwise. I told myself that Monday was the day that I had to worry about it and that I should not worry about it now. So, I did not think about it, and it was not perfect but there was a big improvement. Weekends are usually the hardest for me not to pick, usually because I have a lot of attention on myself without much structure, and I see people when I choose to and I don't have to see anyone. It is possible for me to stay home for forty-eight hours and pick all the time, and this weekend I hardly did it.

THERAPIST: In fact, I am pleased that you were able to do some picking on Tuesday and that you did not completely stop picking, apart from Monday.

Conventionally, a therapist is tempted to congratulate the client when she reports marked improvement. However, this therapist resisted that temptation, because to have praised the client for not picking would have thrown the thrust of treatment back into "You must not pick." Instead, the therapist's comment was consistent with a direction that had brought some results, i.e., the strategy of "Never drop a winning game." Also consistent with the intervention, the therapist shifted to the importance of improving slowly, explaining that change that occurs slowly is more likely to endure.

Laura also had said that she found this past weekend less stressful than usual and that she assumed this might explain the decrease in picking. You may recall that this explanation contradicted what Laura had said previously, that it was when she was under stress that she picked less and that weekends were worse because of the absence of demand. It is possible that she had not anticipated such a rapid change in her problem and did not relate the change to such a seemingly innocuous assignment, and therefore explained the change to the commonsense notion that she was under less stress.

One of the observers, John Weakland (J.W.), entered the room to comment on her explanation.

J.W.: I am relieved; in fact we are all relieved in the back room because you are mitigating the drastic change in the level of your picking at your face by saying that there have been some unusual circumstances and there have been ups and downs, so the improvement in the last week may not be as big as it looks like; it may just be something temporary. That is good. But at the same time, I don't know how we can emphasize enough that there is this danger of moving too fast, and you should keep it in mind so that you can guard against not getting carried away in a rush. So, I think that this cannot be overemphasized, and it is something that people naturally tend to sort of look through or move right past it in their hope for progress. But if you want something that is solid enough and not just buildup to a let-down, you've got to hold yourself and go slow on this thing.

LAURA: OK.

Weakland's explanation to Laura for the need to improve slowly was a reiteration of the comment made by the therapist, a continuation of the strategy, "You should pick at your face." This kind of intervention also implied to the client that what she had done was to set in motion a "healing" that would proceed on its own, requiring her constant attention to holding it back. It was a reversal of the common injunction that the client must continuously struggle to overcome the problem, which is a more pessimistic notion.

LAURA: I think it makes sense to take it one step at a time, because I have had this problem for many years. It probably has protected me from other things, but now it is time to give it up. One thing that I am going to have to deal with a lot better is my assertiveness, which is something, in my line of work, that I need to master. Especially for women, this is important.

THERAPIST: Having said all that we have, we don't want to give you a new assignment. We don't even want you to repeat the old one.

LAURA: (Surprised) Oh! OK.

THERAPIST: However, if in your best judgment *you* think that it could be useful and not too much, you could repeat it just once.

LAURA: I can only do it once a week anyway; right?

THERAPIST: Use your judgment as to whether it would not be pushing things too fast and it would be useful. The other thing is that we would like you to observe how, in particular, you are having trouble being assertive. Again, we leave it up to you in which context you want to do the observing, whether at work or in your own life. This is not related to the picking of your face.

LAURA: OK.

Session Four

THERAPIST: We had left it up to you whether you wanted to improve a notch or keep it the same. How did it go in the last two weeks?

LAURA: Well, I was kind of worried because I had two weeks. When I saw you last, my skin was in a pretty good mode, but I was afraid I would scratch it to where I would wreck it again. And then, for ten days I didn't scratch it hardly at all, although I worried about it. I was worried it would break out, so I was in a lot of anxiety, but the appearance was really good for many days, and I did not scratch it. Then, last Saturday, I did scratch it but felt so much better after doing it. I think I was just so worried that after I did it I realized it was not as bad as I had thought it would be. I felt relieved. And then in the last few days it is all healed up again. It was very minor scratching. It was not like serious digging and scratching; it was light scratching, and by now it is clearing up really well. So I had almost two good weeks of just an occasional episode here and there. I *felt* a lot of anxiety about it but did not *act* on a lot of my impulses.

THERAPIST: Is that different from what you would have done before?

LAURA: Yes.

THERAPIST: Are you aware of how you were able to do that?

Note that the therapist didn't ask, "How were you able to do that?" Putting the question in that form runs the risk of the client responding with some denial of having actively done anything, perhaps being the passive recipient of some external influence: "Oh, I didn't do anything. It just happened."

But put in the form of "Are you aware . . . ?" makes a no into a yes response, yes in the sense that "I did do something but am not aware of how" (our thanks to Milton Erickson for this very useful form of influential language).

LAURA: I made a real effort to have an organized schedule and have to see people, and that made it easier to not scratch my face. "You know, you have to see Judith tomorrow," or having a company meeting and having to make a presentation for the president. "You don't want to sit in that room with blemishes on your face." But I felt so much anxiety about it that I felt almost as bad as if I had done it!

THERAPIST: This is going to sound strange, but I am really pleased to hear that you are at least hanging on to the anxiety part of your scratching your face. At least you are not moving so fast both on the behavior *and* anxiety part.

LAURA: Oh! That makes sense.

THERAPIST: It is one way in which you can still control the speed at which you improve this problem. One step at a time. You have chosen to start with the behavior, not doing it, and then the anxiety will probably follow.

LAURA: OK. Instead of looking at totally controlling the scratching it would be more the case of being more or less in control but not control versus lack of control. That would be good. Because I have noticed that I have this problem that if I have just one pimple and I scratch at it, I feel as bad as if I had done this horrible thing; I make everything good or everything bad, and it affects my whole mood and how I approach everything. One doughnut and the whole day is gone!

You know, in fact, there have been a lot of days where I have gotten up and felt really relieved, like I look normal and it has been really neat. I don't look strange or have to do bizarre things in the morning to get the swelling down. It is a really different kind of life, almost. It is very comforting. It's nice to be able to jog and run into people you know and not be afraid and have to cover my face.

Later in the session, Laura talked about the problem of lack of assertiveness. She reported that, out of the blue, she had called her mother, who had been threatening to make a visit in the near future with little or no notice. Laura said that in the past she would listen passively and not mention that she wanted some sufficient notice before a visit. This time, she was surprised to find herself telling her mother that she did not want to be surprised by a visit and that she needed at least two weeks notice rather than getting an unexpected phone call from the airport announcing she had just arrived.

Again, with a client's report of definite improvement, the therapist responded with the concern that Laura might be improving too fast. Laura responded by saying, "Well, it is going to take some practice, and I'd better start soon!"

The remainder of the session involved an assessment of where the problem stood at that point; much of this kind of discussion occurs when a client has been reporting definite and marked change. In many cases, a client will make such a report even though the problem, by objective standards, is not completely gone. We are more interested in whether the degree of improvement is to the *client's* satisfaction, not to our satisfaction; in other words, does the client still regard any residual of her trouble as a *problem*, or not? If she does, we will proceed with the therapy; if she does not, we check to see if the client is ready to terminate therapy. If the client does wish to termi-

nate, we graciously accede to the client's values, although, when possible, we leave the door open to ad hoc continuation.

Laura was pleased that she could now leave her house in the
mornings without the cumbersome and time-consuming rituals
regarding her appearance. For her, this was the criterion of success,
and thus she and the therapist agreed on terminating therapy.
Because she had used only four sessions, she was told that she had
six sessions in the bank and that she could draw on any or all of
them should the need arise.

Follow-Up

As is our custom, we did a follow-up three months after Laura's last
session. At that time she said she was not picking at her face as
much, once or twice a month at the most and sometimes less. She
added that she had lost some weight and, overall, felt she had
improved a lot. She had been more assertive with her family, setting up rules with her mother with which she felt more comfortable.

At our follow-up one year after the last appointment, Laura
reported that she still picked a little at her face but not to the point
where she had trouble leaving her house. She would go for several
weeks at a time without any picking. She felt more confident in herself and, as a mark of this, no longer avoided her friends. She felt
the relationship with her mother was much better. Finally, she had
not felt the need for any further therapy.

With Laura and many clients, enlisting their motivation to change
has not presented any formidable task. Usually we take pains to
note clients' frame of reference and incorporate that perspective in
the framing we present to explain why a shift away from what they
have been doing is a logical necessity and, therefore, calls for an
unorthodox but logical approach to their problems.

However, there are a number of clients who have presented a
considerable challenge to this aspect of our therapy, that of gaining

their compliance to do something different from what they had been doing about the problem. Our failure to encourage clients to make this shift is responsible for a significant percentage of our failure cases.

The following chapter pursues the subject of our failure to persuade some clients to take a different path from the one they had been following in their futile efforts to resolve their complaint.

9

Where Do We Go from Here?

We have been in the custom of reviewing cases that didn't work out to see what, if we had the cases to do over again, we would have done differently. Our best assessment has yielded a few elements that seem to be most outstanding when cases have failed.

WHAT'S THE PROBLEM?

Earlier in our work, we had difficulty obtaining a clear statement of the client's complaint. There had been cases at the Brief Therapy Center that, by research design, we had to terminate at the end of ten sessions and for which at termination we had no clear idea as to exactly what the client's problem was! Thus we did not get to the point of eliciting the client's attempts to deal with whatever the problem was and to intervene in that attempt.

Over time, we improved at eliciting clear information, and this factor has been considerably reduced as a contributor to failure. We are usually able to understand the complaint in the first session or so.

LISTEN!

There were and still are other factors in cases that haven't turned out well: our jumping too quickly into suggesting some action to clients before we were clear what attempts they had already made;

and our not recognizing or eliciting clients' position or frame of reference regarding their problem. These factors, too, have become less troublesome over time, mainly because of our continuing reminder to *listen* to the client.

GAINING COMPLIANCE

Finally, there were cases in which we failed not because of any of these aforementioned factors but because we were unable to get the client to accept a change in the approach he had been using in attempting to resolve the problem.

In common terms, we had failed to "sell" the client. This kind of failure was the most common element when therapy was unsuccessful in serious cases; it is also the most frustrating experience for us. When working with most other problems, we have been able to get clear information regarding the complaint and the clients' attempted solution; we have been able to formulate a suggestion and then find some credible explanation for their departing from their customary attempts and, instead, taking an appropriate alternative action. However, in what we have been calling serious or intimidating problems, this last step is more problematic. Our frustration stems from having all the data we feel we need to make a definitive intervention: we know, rather exactly, what, if we could get the clients to make the change, would likely result in some improvement in their problems; yet to our dismay we find we are unable to get them to do it.

Our frustration is even more acute when, after we have carefully framed some rationale for a change in their efforts, clients fully agree with that framing and, further, agree to follow through on a specific suggestion, but return the following session to report they hadn't done it.

Often, the reasons they give for noncompliance are vague, or they give no explanation at all. However, in a few cases, the clients have been explicit, and their explanations are rather similar. They have all felt that any different move on their parts ran too high a risk of worsening the problem, with the potential of leading to a catastrophe.

For example, the parents of a young man who had been labeled schizophrenic were infantilizing him. They were not intending to do so but felt strongly that he needed to know they cared about him, that he was "a part of the family." They tried to convey their caring by delaying their own dinner until he deigned to come downstairs and join them at the dinner table. This might take a half hour or more, with his mother making frequent trips to his room to politely remind him that dinner was ready.

We explained that, thoughtful as this might be on their parts, it ran the risk of burdening him with a responsibility and also of engendering feelings of guilt for holding up their dinner. They fully agreed that this made a lot of sense. They were then instructed to remind him about dinner, once, wait five minutes, and, if he wasn't down by that time, go ahead with their own meal. We asked if there would be any problem in trying that out, and they readily said there wouldn't be. Yet, when they came back, they sheepishly said they hadn't done it. They explained that they still feared he would take their eating without him as rejection, which would throw him into a psychotic break. They added that he had had such a break a year or so before, resulting in a very prolonged hospitalization; their explanation at the time was that he had felt rejected by them.

We know that in intimidating cases there is a realistic concern for catastrophe of one sort or another. In deep depressions it is the fear of suicide or, at least, economic ruin; in anorexia it is the fear of death by starvation or some other calamitous health problem; in paranoia it can be the fear of some unpredictable and outrageous action. At the very least, serious problems occurring with adolescents or young adults raise the fear in their parents of a marginal life for their child, a failed and dependent life. It is a tragedy for parents to see their child suffering, slipping from the mainstream of their peers and raising the threat of being a burden on them for the rest of their lives. For them, it is catastrophic.

Clients may express intense emotions at times: pressured speech, crying, wringing their hands, looking at you pleadingly; at those times it can be difficult for you to keep in mind that the client's suffering stems from the unresolved problem and that your job is to aid the client in resolving it. It can be easy, instead, to get caught up in the emotionality of the client, to shift the focus to the client's emotions. This does not mean that you need to get on with the tasks at hand brusquely, totally ignoring the client's distress. You can graciously acknowledge the client's feelings while still reminding the client of the main purpose of your meeting: "You're understandably upset. Are you too upset to continue where we left off? We can get back to it next time."

THE INTIMIDATED CLIENT

We have, at least for the time being, decided that a strategic factor in motivating clients facing serious problems is that they are intimidated by the presumed fragility of their family member (mainly offspring or spouse). For them, adhering to their attempts at solution is more than "the only reasonable thing to do"; it is the tenuous thread that keeps catastrophe at bay. Although we have succeeded in redirecting many clients from their original direction, we have yet to arrive at a more consistent and reliable way of achieving that shift in all serious cases.

For us, this is the challenge: helping clients overcome or deal with their intimidation so that their usual efforts can be diverted. There are a number of other contexts in which change agents accomplish this diversion; these people also need to get a client to depart from what is logical or instinctive in situations where the client is understandably fearful of a catastrophic result. In flight instruction, for example, the "instinct" is to pull the nose of the plane up in order to gain or maintain altitude, yet this can produce a "stall," with a sudden and frightening drop. The maneuver required to correct the stall is to let the nose drop *down*. (In some types of aircraft, just letting go of the stick, or yoke, will correct the stall, because it is the student's continuing to pull back that maintains the stall and, therefore, the fall.) The student is facing what he or she considers imminent death yet needs to learn to disregard instinct and do what is seemingly illogical.

Other examples of activities involving severe danger are skiing and horseback riding. The student skier, fearful of falling head-first down a steep slope, may "instinctively" lean his body up slope and thereby risk falling. The equestrian student, fearful of falling off the horse, may "instinctively" bend her body forward, leaning over the horse's neck and, by badly altering her center of gravity, fall off the horse. Yet in these activities, the students somehow are trained to go against instinct and to trust what is illogical in the face of catastrophe.

We believe it would be useful to profit from the experiences of these other change agents, who daily face tasks similar to our own. How do they get people who are terrified to follow counterintuitive directives? How did they arrive at these methods? Do they customize their methods for the particular individual student? At the very least, these questions would make for very interesting story swapping.

References and Suggested Readings

Bateson, G., Jackson, D. D., Haley, J., and Weakland, J. H. "The 'Double Bind' Hypothesis of Schizophrenia and Three Party Interaction." In D. D. Jackson (ed.), *The Etiology of Schizophrenia*. New York: Basic Books, 1960.

Cade, B., and O'Hanlon, W. *Brief Guide to Brief Therapy*. New York: Norton, 1993.

Crispo, R., Figueroa, E., and Guelar, D. *Trastornos del Comer* [Eating Disorders]. Barcelona, Spain: Editorial Herder, 1994.

de Shazer, S. *Keys to Solution in Brief Therapy*. New York: Norton, 1985.

Fisch, R. "Sometimes It's Better Not to Let the Right Hand Know What the Left Hand Is Doing." In P. Papp (ed.), *Family Therapy: Full Length Case Studies*. New York: Gardner Press, 1977.

Fisch, R. "Training in the Brief Therapy Model." In H. A. Liddle, D. C. Breulin, and R. C. Schwartz (eds.), *Handbook of Family Therapy Training and Supervision*. New York: Guilford Press, 1988.

Fisch, R. "The Broader Implications of Milton H. Erickson's Work." In S. Lankton (ed.), *The Broader Implications of Ericksonian Therapy*. Ericksonian Monographs, no. 7. New York: Brunner/Mazel, 1990.

Fisch, R. "Basic Elements in the Brief Therapies." In M. F. Hoyt (ed.), *Constructive Therapies*. New York: Guilford Press, 1994.

Fisch, R., Weakland, J. H., and Segal, L. *The Tactics of Change: Doing Therapy Briefly*. San Francisco: Jossey-Bass, 1982.

Gill, L. *Stop—You're Driving Me Crazy!* New York: Simon & Schuster, 1999.

Haley, J. *Uncommon Therapy: The Psychiatric Techniques of Milton H. Erickson, M.D.* New York: Norton, 1973.

Ruesch, J., and Bateson, G. *Communication: The Social Matrix of Psychiatry*. New York: Norton, 1951.

Schlanger, K. "Looking Back, Looking Forward: Reflections in the MRI Mirror." In W. Ray and S. de Shazer (eds.), *Evolving Brief Therapies: Essays in Honor of John H. Weakland*. Atlanta: Geist and Russel, forthcoming.

Schlanger, K., and Anger-Diaz, B. "A Threat of Suicide: The Client's or the Therapist's Problem?" *AFTA Newsletter*, Spring 1996, pp. 10–13.

Schlanger, K., and Anger-Diaz, B. "The Brief Therapy Approach of the Palo Alto Group." In F. Worchel (ed.), *Casebook in Marriage and Family Therapy*. Pacific Grove, Calif.: Brooks/Cole, forthcoming.

Shute, N. "The Drinking Dilemma." *U.S. News and World Report*, Sept. 8, 1997.

Sullivan, H. S. *Schizophrenia as a Human Process*. (H. S. Perry, ed.). New York: Norton, 1962.

Watzlawick, P., Weakland, J. H., and Fisch, R. *Change: Principles of Problem Formation and Problem Resolution*. New York: Norton, 1974.

Watzlawick, P. (ed.). *The Invented Reality*. New York: Norton, 1984.

Weakland, J. H. "Pursuing the Evident into Schizophrenia and Beyond." In M. M. Berger (ed.), *Beyond the Double Bind: Communication and Family Systems, Theories, and Techniques with Schizophrenics*. New York: Brunner/Mazel, 1978.

Weakland, J. H., and Fisch, R. "A Case of Minimal Brain Damage Treated With Brief Psychotherapy." In D. M. Ross and S. A. Ross (eds.), *Hyperactivity: Research, Theory and Action*. New York: Wiley, 1976.

Weakland, J. H., and Fisch, R. "Brief Therapy—MRI Style." In S. Budman, M. F. Hoyt, and S. Friedman (eds.), *The First Session in Brief Therapy*. New York: Guilford Press, 1992.

Weiner-Davis, M. *Divorce Busting*. New York: Simon & Schuster, 1992.

Wittezaele, J. J., and Garcia, T. *A la Recherche de L'Ecole de Palo Alto*. France: Editions du Seuil, 1992.

About the Authors

RICHARD FISCH, M.D., is a psychiatrist who has been practicing in Palo Alto since 1958, after having completed a psychiatric residency at the Sheppard and Enoch Pratt Hospital, where Harry Stack Sullivan had done his earlier work. Among his educational experiences, Fisch values his years at the Bronx High School of Science in New York ("That's where I learned how to learn") and at Colby College in Maine, where he was greatly influenced by his instructor in anthropology, Dr. Kingsley Birge. Fisch received his medical training at the New York Medical College after a short stint at Columbia University School of Anthropology.

Fisch was introduced to family therapy through training he took in 1960 with Virginia Satir at the Mental Research Institute. He became a research associate there in 1961, and later a senior research fellow. Together with his colleagues at the institute, John Weakland and Paul Watzlawick, Fisch organized the clinical research project, the Brief Therapy Center, in 1966, which has continued uninterrupted to this day.

Fisch has four children living in disparate parts of the country: David in North Carolina, Amy in Los Angeles, Sara in San Francisco, and Ben in Salinas. For recreation, Fisch enjoys flying and is an instrument-rated pilot; he is also addicted to dark chocolate.

KARIN SCHLANGER, MFCC, is originally from Buenos Aires, Argentina. She studied clinical psychology and received her Licenciatura degree from the Universidad de Buenos Aires in 1982, where she first learned about the Mental Research Institute. She moved to Palo Alto in 1983 and worked with the Center for the Treatment of Eating Disorders using the Palo Alto approach.

Schlanger returned to school, receiving a degree in clinical psychology in 1987 and licensure in 1991. During her years of internship, she worked with the Latino population and consulted at San Francisco General Hospital, treating clients who were noncompliant with their medical treatment. Later, in her work at a halfway house, she applied principles of brief therapy to the treatment of clients labeled schizophrenic and manic depressive.

Schlanger is in private practice and recently became the assistant director of the Brief Therapy Center. She is founder and codirector of the Latino Brief Therapy Center. This Center, in partnership with a magnet school in East Palo Alto, recently received a grant, *una mano amiga* ("a friendly hand"), to meet the special needs of at-risk Latino families and children.

Because Schlanger speaks five languages—Spanish, English, French, Italian, and German—she is able to conduct trainings in Europe and Latin America as well as the United States. She is also an adjunct professor at the University of San Francisco.

The rest of her time is spent with her two sons—Andreas, four, and Felipe, eight—and her husband, David.

Index